In appreciation
for
your dedication
to
the children
of
Temple Beth El SOC

Teach Them Diligently

A Midrash on the Jewish Educator's Year

Bonnie K. Stevens

BEHRMAN HOUSE INC
www.behrmanhouse.com

Book and cover design: Masters Group Design, Inc.

Editor: Anne Berman-Waldorf

Copyeditor: Bryna Fischer

Project Manager: Terry S. Kaye

Behrman House, Inc.
11 Edison Place
Springfield, NJ 07081
www.behrmanhouse.com

Library of Congress Cataloging-in-Publication Data

Stevens, Bonnie Klomp.
Teach them diligently : a midrash on the Jewish educator's year / Bonnie K. Stevens.
   p. cm.
Includes bibliographical references and index.
ISBN-10: 0-87441-145-9
ISBN-13: 978-0-87441-145-4
1. Fasts and feasts—Judaism—Study and teaching (Elementary) 2. Jewish religious education of children. I. Title.

   BM690.S74 2005
   296.6'8—dc22

                                        2005000665

Manufactured in the United States of America

In memory of Esther Levow Anderson,
my mother and first teacher

❖❖❖ ACKNOWLEDGMENTS ❖❖❖

Many people have made important contributions to *Teach Them Diligently*. I am grateful to David Behrman for his initial interest in the manuscript and to Terry Kaye for her help in seeing the book through the final stages of production. Anne Berman-Waldorf, the Director of Lifelong Education at Congregation Beth Chaim in Princeton Junction, New Jersey, acted as an editor for Behrman House, reading the entire manuscript and making a number of helpful suggestions. Bryna Fischer ably copyedited the manuscript. I also very much appreciate the generous help provided by several Jewish educators and other experts who reviewed all or part of the manuscript, contributed many valuable ideas, and suggested resources: Rabbi Judith Bluestein, Dr. Sherry Feinstein, Sarah Gershone, Eileen Kollins of the Jewish Community Federation of Cleveland, Bernice Schotten, and Barbara Shapiro of the Jewish Education Center of Cleveland.

Over the past fifteen years, I have taught at several schools and synagogues in various parts of the country. At all of these places, I have learned a great deal from the students, parents, and colleagues with whom I have worked; I will always have a special affection for and particularly deep debts to the families of Mount Zion Temple in Sioux Falls, South Dakota, where I was the religious school principal for five years.

Most of all, I am grateful to my husband, Dennis, and to our daughters, Sarah and Rachel. Through every stage of the writing and editing of this book, they have given freely of their time and insight, reading and rereading various versions of the manuscript and suggesting countless additions and improvements. It is an understatement to say that I could not have completed this book without their help and encouragement. For us, Jewish education has always been a family undertaking, a shared commitment. I have many precious memories of days when we all worked together to make props and costumes for religious-school plays, and of nights when we all stayed up late to complete the final preparations for a religious-school holiday celebration. There are many excellent reasons for teaching religious school; for me, one of the most compelling is that it offers a family frequent opportunities to grow closer through working on worthwhile projects together. For their help on all those projects, and for their help with this book, I can never thank Dennis, Sarah, and Rachel enough.

Table of Contents

Introduction

THE JEWISH EDUCATOR'S YEAR

Several years ago, on a warm Saturday night late in May, I saw the connection for the first time. It was the night before the last day of religious school; as usual, I was running late. I had vowed that this year would be different, that this time I'd plan everything so carefully and start preparing so far in advance that by Saturday there would be nothing left to do but to take one final, smug look at my checklist. But the last-minute delays and complications had popped up, as they always seem to do, and here it was, well after midnight, and I still hadn't filled out the students' certificates of achievement. Picking up the first certificate and writing the year on the designated line, I reflected that at least Jewish educators get one break: When filling out end-of-the-year certificates, we can save a few seconds. No need to bother with "2001–2002," or whatever the secular academic year might be. Just four digits—in this case, 5762—covered our school year precisely.

That's when I first became intrigued by the correspondence between the Hebrew year and the academic year. Obviously, it can't be anything but coincidence; the ancient Jewish calendar was not designed to accommodate our contemporary school schedule. But I continue to find it a fortunate, rich, suggestive coincidence.

We begin our school year and our new Jewish year at the same time, with a full, splendid season. The High Holy Days command us to look back at the past year, to think about what we did well and what we wish we'd done differently, to put mistakes behind us, to set new goals, and to fix our thoughts on the future. Then come Sukkot and Simḥat Torah, tempting us with an image of the harvest our efforts will eventually yield, inviting us to clasp the Torah to our hearts and to rejoice as we move ahead. Who could possibly imagine a better way for Jewish teachers to begin a new year of learning? Finally, we end our school year with Shavuot—with a reaffirmation of our commitment to the mitzvot, with a celebration of the first fruits of our labors, with a dream of the fuller harvest yet to come. The symmetry and symbolism of the fall holidays and Shavuot provide us with the perfect metaphor for the Jewish teacher's year, reminding us of the eternal cycle of beginning and fulfillment, of the constant movement from promise to promise, and of our enduring commitment to begin again.

And between Rosh Hashanah and Shavuot, what an amazing series of holidays we have, each reminding us of our direction and purpose as Jewish educators. Ḥanukkah speaks to us of the need to help our students become modern Maccabees who have a sense of Jewish identity so firm that they can withstand the temptations of assimilation and secularization, steadfast in their loyalty to the Jewish community. Ḥanukkah also reminds us, as teachers, of the need to be sensitive to the differences in belief and practice within that community and, sometimes, within our students' own families. Tu B'Shevat underscores the teacher's role as cultivator, taking on the usually far-from-glamorous task of nurturing even when we know we may never see the fruits that spring from the seeds we plant. It reminds us that the teacher is both a practical, conscientious worker attending to the details of preparing each day's lesson and a dreamer guided by a vision of what is to come.

Traditional ways of observing Purim show us how learning can be enhanced by music, drama, and other arts. Purim also reminds us that play and high spirits have a part in Jewish education—and the good humor associated with the holiday suggests ways of keeping our balance when high spirits get out of hand. Passover provides us with a classic textbook, the Haggadah, which impresses on us the role questions play in education, the importance of the family, and the value of continually returning to our basic texts. It also impresses upon us both the absolute necessity of passing on our heritage and the inevitable difficulty of doing so. Pharaoh needed to suffer through ten plagues before he learned a simple lesson; once he learned it, he promptly forgot it. And the people of Israel, witnesses to countless miracles, nevertheless grumbled and doubted and yearned to go back to Egypt. Even God, equipped with audio-visual aids more spectacular than any the most creative teacher could devise, found education a hard, frustrating job—and, sometimes, a heartbreaking one. What does that tell us about the difficulty of the task we face as Jewish educators, about the frustrations we're bound to encounter? What hope and comfort does it offer us on days when we feel like just giving up?

Year after year, we teach our students about these holidays. We use the holidays to introduce students to central Jewish beliefs, pivotal events in our people's history, and ideas that we hope will guide their lives and help them become better Jews. Perhaps we can benefit from reexamining the holidays from a teacher's perspective. What do they tell us about our mission as educators? How can they help us find the best ways of reaching our students? What encouragement do they offer us? Can we add to our interpretations of these holidays in ways that meet our own special needs, creating an educator's midrash that will help us become better teachers and find in our work a source for our own spiritual renewal?

This book is organized around the major Jewish holidays, but it does not focus on explaining those holidays or on exploring approaches to teaching them. There are already many excellent books, websites, teachers' manuals, and other resources available to teachers looking for specific suggestions about how to teach the holidays. This book takes a different approach by reflecting on how each holiday suggests themes and ideas that can inform our teaching—our relationship to our students, our understanding of what we do, our goals and frustrations, the rewards we hope to find. It offers some general principles, some practical advice, some anecdotes, some humor, lots of encouragement. Some teachers might choose to read the entire book on their own during the summer as one way of preparing for the coming year; alternatively, some religious school staffs might decide to read the book together throughout the year, using a given chapter as a discussion focus at faculty development sessions as the corresponding holiday approaches. I hope that each chapter honestly acknowledges the challenges we face day after day, without losing sight of the joys that keep us coming back to the classroom year after year. I hope that each chapter offers something of value both to new teachers, unsure of what lies ahead, and to veterans who sometimes doubt how much they've accomplished during the long years behind them.

We share the September-to-May year with secular schools and with schools that teach other faiths. But the Jewish holidays endow our school year with a special significance and dignity. Taking yet another look at the symbols, customs, and themes of those familiar holidays can help us see our work in a new way; it can help us do that work more effectively and joyfully. As teachers, we know how easy it is to get completely caught up in the demands of the moment. We worry about tomorrow's lesson plan, about the project our students will do during the second hour of class, about how we'll handle the ten minutes remaining before assembly. Taking a step back and looking at the year as a whole, in the context of our holidays, can help us see how all the many moments come together to form an eternally meaningful and beautiful pattern.

Our Jewish school year is framed by sacred days, filled with and shaped by them. Perhaps taking yet another look at these holidays can guide us toward a fuller appreciation of the sanctity of our work and help us make every school year a year of learning, deepened commitment, joy, and spiritual growth—for all of our students, and for all of us. ❀

1. The Fall Holidays

LOOKING BACK, SETTING GOALS, AND MOVING AHEAD

Now is the time to let the mind
search backwards like the raven loosed
to see what can feed us. Now,
the time to cast the mind forward
to chart an aerial map of the months.

—Marge Piercy, "Coming upon September,"
Eight Chambers of the Heart

Our year begins with the sound of the shofar, jolting us to attention; with a taste of sweetness; with white Torah covers symbolic of a new beginning; with a call to *t'shuvah*, to return. For most of us, fall is the time when we literally return to our classrooms after a summer of rest and preparation. But *t'shuvah*, as we often tell our students, is more than a simple process of going back to some point we've already reached in the past. Ideally, *t'shuvah* allows us to learn from our past and move into the future, providing us with firm grounds for believing that what is yet to come will be better than what lies behind. As teachers, we can see this season of *t'shuvah* as a time for searching and sometimes painful, sometimes joyful reflection. People speak of "wiping the slate clean"; every fall, we teachers can picture ourselves wiping our blackboards—or whiteboards—clean of last year's regrets. We can set new goals, resolving to make this fresh, bright year an even better one for our students and for ourselves.

For teachers, the work of *t'shuvah* begins before the High Holy Days arrive. It may begin on Shavuot, when we leave the assembly on the last day of religious school already thinking about what we'll do differently next year. It may continue throughout the summer, as we study our textbooks and chart out a sequence of lessons. And it may reach a climax on the first day of class, when we invite our students to join us in envisioning what the coming year might be. Whenever our process of *t'shuvah* begins, and however long it lasts, the themes and images of the fall holidays provide us with invaluable guidance.

Rosh Hashanah: Looking Both Ways

If you've taught religious school before, chances are you've had your students do some version of the High Holy Days activity I'm about to describe. If you're just starting, chances are you'll have them do it before long. This one is a classic, and for good reason.

For the first part of the activity, we give our students slips of paper and markers or pencils. We ask them to think back on the past year and to write or draw about mistakes they've made, people they've hurt, times they wish they'd behaved differently. Are there people to whom our students should apologize or actions they should take to make up for things they've done wrong? After they've finished, we have our students rip their papers into tiny pieces. As we pass around a wastebasket, we speak reassuring words: There, we say. It's good to remember that we haven't always been as kind or helpful as we'd like. And it's important to resolve to apologize and make amends. But now that you've admitted to your mistakes and decided to do whatever it takes to set things right, you can put the mistakes behind you. You can make this fresh, new year better.

Next, we give our students clean slips of paper and invite them to draw or write about goals for the coming year. Some goals may be general—"I'll be nicer," "I'll help more." Others may be specific—"I'll try not to yell at my sister," "I'll take the trash out on Wednesdays." Then we ask students to tape their papers inside their notebook covers, or seal the papers in envelopes we'll give back at the end of the year. One fall, my students and I put our envelopes in a small silver gift bag and left it sitting on my desk all year, a quiet reminder of the goals we'd set.

It's a good activity. It gives students concrete images of the processes of repentance and renewal. It helps them understand some steps involved in *t'shuvah*—confessing, apologizing and making amends, resolving to do better, moving ahead.

It's a good activity for teachers, too. At some point—or several points—before the school year begins, we can benefit from looking back. It helps to do ourselves what we ask of our students—to actually write things down.

I like to set aside an evening several weeks before school begins, load up the Debbie Friedman CDs, and take out three yellow pads. On the first pad, I take notes about last year's low points—classes that fell flat, lessons that didn't connect with the students, discipline problems I wish I'd handled differently, opportunities I missed. On the second pad, I take notes about high points—moments when students' eyes widened with understanding, times we worked together happily and effectively, days their accomplishments exceeded expectations and left us all smiling.

I take a break, read over all the notes again, and look for patterns. Did a class fall short because I didn't prepare enough, or when I overprepared, fell in love with my own lesson plan, and couldn't adjust when students didn't respond as I'd expected? Did students' eyes glaze over because I'd packed too much material into a session or because I hadn't made the lesson challenging enough to hold their interest? Did discipline problems arise because I didn't help the class establish guidelines for behavior, or because the guidelines we did set were too strict, too lax, or inappropriate for students their age?

I also ask myself what the good days had in common. Did classes go well when I moved quickly from one activity to another, or when I put aside planned activities to let students linger on a topic they found especially interesting? Did students participate more when we explored a text in depth, or when we used the text as a starting point that let them talk about their experiences? Did discipline problems ease when I took aside disruptive students and talked to them seriously about their behavior, or when a joking reprimand nudged them to stop fooling around and get involved in class?

Inevitably, I also ask myself another question: Why did some approaches work beautifully one day and bomb utterly the next? We can't be too hard on ourselves when we go over our lists; perfection should never be among a teacher's goals. No technique works every time, and there are days when Solomon himself couldn't figure out a way to reach our students, even if he had David backing him up on harp and Miriam punctuating his jokes with tambourine rim shots. Many of us teach on Sunday mornings, when students may come fresh from sleepovers that have left them droopy and sullen, with barely enough energy to grasp their pencils. Or we may see our students on weekday afternoons or evenings when they're already frazzled after a long day, worried about homework they still have to do or tests they'll take in public school tomorrow, or resentful about soccer games or television shows they're missing. When we examine our lists, it's important to be honest about our mistakes but equally important to remember most Jewish educators today teach at less-than-ideal times and under difficult circumstances. When a class fizzles, it may not be our fault (or not entirely our fault); when a class soars, we can justly feel we've beaten the odds and scored a real victory.

After evaluating the past year, it's time to set to work on the third yellow pad. How can we learn from and avoid last year's mistakes? How can we learn from and build on last year's successes so that the coming year will be more consistently satisfying? What will our goals be?

Of course, our school's curriculum and the organization to which our synagogue belongs have much to say about those goals—about the subjects our students will study, the texts they'll use, the knowledge and skills they should master. Even so, we have great freedom, great responsibility. We'll be the ones to decide how each lesson is structured, to establish the atmosphere in our classrooms, to decide how to respond to the many opportunities and challenges that arise. So we need to think rigorously about our personal goals.

Many goals may emerge from our examination of the past year. If looking back convinced us our classes often lacked structure and purpose, we may set the goal of preparing more thoroughly and looking for a central theme to unify each session. If classes often felt rigid and hurried, we may decide to make lesson plans more flexible, leaving room for spontaneity. If we've discovered our best discussions focused on close analysis of texts, we may choose to begin each class by looking at a brief passage from the weekly Torah portion. If we're encouraged by memories of times when students talked eagerly about connections between a text and their own lives, we may resolve to urge them to draw such connections whenever we study a text together.

Some goals will be academic; others will relate to students' attitudes. We want our students to gain knowledge and skills, but also want them to enjoy their time with us and to develop positive feelings about Judaism. It's easy to overemphasize one sort of goal at the expense of the other. There's the danger of making classes so narrowly focused on covering material that our students hide in the basement when it's time to go to religious school; there's also the danger of being so afraid of boring students that we succeed at entertaining them but fail to teach them much. If reviewing the past year makes us suspect we have a tendency in one direction or the other, we can compensate for that tendency when planning the year to come. The chapter on Purim says more about balancing the need to make religious school a pleasant experience for our students with the need to help them build the solid knowledge of Judaism that provides a sure foundation for lifelong commitment.

We also seek a balance between specific goals and larger ones. Some specific goals are set by our curriculum; others we set ourselves. For example, the curriculum may decide we'll teach a children's version of Prophets and Writings. Looking back at confusions that persisted throughout the past year, we may decide to spend more time introducing the idea of prophecy; remembering an especially enjoyable lesson, we may decide that this time, after asking students to write stories to illustrate favorite proverbs, we'll invite them to develop their stories into skits for a school assembly. Setting specific goals helps us focus on central concepts we want to stress, and gives us almost-guaranteed high points to look forward to.

If we measure success only in terms of specific goals, however, we risk overlooking our true achievements. "If there's one thing my students are going to learn this year," we say, voices sharpening with determination, "it's *this*. Whatever else they learn or don't learn, they *will* learn *this*." One year, our confirmation class teacher set the goal of teaching his students the Hebrew names of the books of the Torah. It bothered him that even after bar and bat mitzvah, students still referred to the books by their Greek names; this year, he vowed, his students *would* learn the Hebrew names, and remember them.

He's an excellent teacher, and he did his job well. In September, he put up a striking bulletin board about the Hebrew names of the books of the Torah. He taught his students to call out the names without hesitation, drew them into lively discussions about differences between Jewish and Christian rationales for naming the books, and reviewed often. Eventually, when it was clear the students had learned the Hebrew names so well that they could never forget them, he put up a new bulletin board. A month or so later, he raised the subject again. The students looked at him blankly. Oh, yeah, one finally said. They'd talked about that. It was cool, the way Genesis and Exodus and those other books had Hebrew names, too. Darn. What *were* those names? Not one student could remember a single name.

Those are the days when we stagger out of religious school clutching our book bags limply, gasping for air, wondering why God bothered to put us on this planet when our existence clearly serves no purpose. If we focus only on specific goals, we experience such days often. We can be confident that our students will gain a great deal from a class that's well planned and well presented, but we can't always predict which particular facts they'll remember and which they'll forget. Indeed, students sometimes seem born with a mysterious ability for figuring out the one thing we most want them to learn, putting up impenetrable barriers, and not learning it.

If we focus on larger goals as well, we can protect ourselves against such disappointments. That same year, the same teacher's class got into an unplanned discussion. They started with a Talmudic passage relating to idolatry; the teacher then asked his students to think of forms of idolatry in today's world, and one suggested that good luck charms are like idols. The teacher agreed, saying it's contrary to Judaism to think a physical object can make good things happen or protect us from harm.

Suddenly, the discussion got livelier. Over half the students, it turned out, carried good luck charms, and they vigorously defended their right to do so. One girl—I'll call her Becky—grew especially adamant. She had a lucky coin that she'd found when she was a little girl and carried in her pocket or purse every day; she'd feel nervous about going anywhere without it. She didn't see anything wrong with that and didn't intend to stop. The teacher said, gently, that he understood how she felt and that a habit she'd had for so long would be hard to break. Probably, the first time she left home without her lucky coin, she'd feel uneasy and strange. Even so, he urged her to think about it. Believing a coin could control her life just wasn't a Jewish thing to do.

Becky shrugged his comments off. Even if the coin didn't have magical powers, she said, it made her feel confident—what's un-Jewish about that? When the teacher tried again, she just shook her head. The teacher sighed in resignation. That's one more student I didn't reach, he thought.

Several months later, he opened class in his usual way, by inviting each student to talk about one thing he or she had done during the past week. When Becky's turn came, she hesitated, then said, "I threw my lucky coin away four days ago. I decided carrying a lucky charm isn't a Jewish thing to do."

When the teacher told me this story, we marveled at it together. He'd thought the discussion had made no impression on Becky, but clearly it had touched her so deeply that she'd thought about it for months. And while a good luck charm might not seem significant in itself, a Jewish young person had broken a long-standing habit and given up something that meant a great deal to her because she'd decided keeping it wasn't a Jewish thing to do. That was hugely significant. That might mean that from now on she'd be more likely to look at her other decisions in a Jewish context; that might influence her entire life. Getting Becky to give up her good luck charm might have been the single most important thing that teacher accomplished all year.

And yet he'd never set the goal of persuading his students to give up their good luck charms. He hadn't even known they carried good luck charms. Did that mean his goals were irrelevant to his accomplishment? Not at all. Becky's decision was directly related to several general goals he'd set for the year—to listen to students carefully, to treat their opinions respectfully no matter how much he disagreed, to stay flexible enough to let students help determine the direction discussions took, and to help them see how Judaism could guide decisions in their day-to-day lives. This particular success took him by surprise. Given the larger goals he'd established for the year, however, and his care in making them shape every class, it really wasn't surprising at all.

So we turn from our yellow pads, or computers, or whatever aids we've used, and we fix our attention on the future. We may share some of our reflections about the past year and some of our plans for the next one with colleagues, mentors, or supervisors. We look over our list of goals, taking them seriously but knowing the coming year won't turn out exactly as planned. Sometimes, we'll fall short of our goals; sometimes, we'll surpass them; often, we won't be able to figure out why. Even so, analyzing the past year and setting goals for the new one is bound to make us better teachers—more determined to improve, more conscious of what we're doing and why. We can now rip up the regret-heavy pages recording last year's disappointments—we're finished with those mistakes. We can move on. Perhaps we should conclude the exercise with apples and honey—or a fat-free brownie, if we prefer. We've done our best to make the new year sweet. We deserve a reward.

Yom Kippur: Exchanging Forgiveness

Other High Holy Day traditions can also guide us as we begin our new year. As we all know, the Days of Awe are a time for forgiving those who have wronged us and asking for forgiveness from those we ourselves have wronged. For members of a religious school staff, this exchange of forgiveness can be vital. We care deeply about what we do—otherwise, we wouldn't do it at all, because heaven knows the pay isn't good, and often there's no pay at all; often, we dig into our own pockets to pay for snacks and stickers and extra art supplies. The other teachers share our dedication but may not share our opinions. We get into heated discussions at teachers' meetings, and sometimes we step on each other's feelings: debates about curriculum or even about games at the Purim carnival can turn, suddenly, into debates about another teacher's understanding of Judaism. As teachers, we have a special need to take to heart our own lessons about exchanging forgiveness before starting a new year.

It can be hard on our egos, but it works. This is yet another time when being guided by our tradition's wisdom makes supremely good sense. Not long ago, I learned that lesson again, after a seemingly tiny incident at a Shabbat family potluck. Several preschoolers started chasing each other around during the after-dinner singing. They weren't making much noise—not yet—but it was distracting, and I feared it would get worse. So I walked over to each child individually and quietly told him or her to sit down. The children obeyed, and the singing continued undisturbed. As far as I was concerned, I'd handled the situation effectively and tactfully.

But then I got a call from one preschooler's mother, a teacher at our religious school. As far as she was concerned, I'd been out of line—I'd undermined her authority by disciplining her child in her presence. The conversation went on for some time, with many assertions of her rights as a parent and my responsibilities as a principal. She said things about being too repressive, and I said things about being too indulgent; we came dangerously close to challenging each other not only as teachers but also as parents. Neither of us would concede anything. Finally, we agreed to disagree, declared we were still friends, and hung up.

After that, when we saw each other at school or services, we were elaborately polite. At teachers' meetings, we carefully prefaced disagreements with comments about how much we respected the other person's opinions. The tension never lifted. We could still work together, but we no longer enjoyed it; obviously, we no longer liked each other much.

Fall came, and as usual I taught my students about exchanging forgiveness with people with whom we'd had conflicts during the past year. This time, the lesson felt poignant, because I couldn't stop thinking about the woman in the classroom down the hall, the woman I, in fact, respected greatly as a fine teacher and devoted mother. Kol Nidrei fell on a Sunday night that year; we had only hours left. I let my students go early, waited outside her door, went into her classroom as soon as her students left, and apologized. I couldn't say my actions were wrong—to this day, I honestly don't believe they were—but I knew I'd lost my temper and said harsh things. I could sincerely say I was sorry for that, and for hurting her feelings. She looked very surprised and enormously relieved. She'd felt bad about the conversation, too, she said, and she too was sorry. We forgave each other whole-heartedly, hugged briefly, felt awkward together, chatted about nothing for a moment, and went on our ways. Ever since, things have been fine. We can disagree without first having to say how much we respect each other. We like each other again.

Many of us make a point of exchanging forgiveness with family members during the Days of Awe. Maybe we should make a point of exchanging forgiveness with fellow teachers, too. It feels cleansing, it feels liberating—it feels exactly the way Yom Kippur is supposed to feel. And it's not as hard as we think it's going to be. No Jewish teacher worth his or her salt can turn us down if we ask for forgiveness during the Days of Awe. So let's say whatever is needed to erase last year's tensions; let's express the respect and affection we truly feel for one another; and let's move ahead unburdened, united in our efforts to do the work that means so much to all of us.

Sukkot: Shelter, Symbols, Stars

The sukkah is a powerful metaphor for the Jewish classroom. It is, first of all, a shelter, a place that protects our students and us.

Here, students say things they might not dare to say in public school, ask questions they might not dare to ask gentile teachers in front of gentile friends. We decorate the sukkah with symbols of the harvest; we decorate our classrooms with symbols of our heritage. But neither the sukkah nor the Jewish classroom is closed off from the world. We leave the roof of the sukkah open, so we can gaze at the stars and feel the wonder of Creation. The Jewish classroom, too, is left open: to wonder, to possibility, to visions of all our students and we might accomplish in this world.

It's easy to dismiss preparing the classroom as our least important beginning-of-the-year task. I've heard teachers brag about how inept they are at putting up bulletin boards and how little they care about it. In some ways, the physical appearance of a classroom indeed seems trivial. If our words are brilliant, what does it matter what our classrooms look like?

I favor squandering many hours of summer on bulletin boards. I have no artistic ability—I can't draw a cat to save my life—but even I can cut pictures out of old Jewish calendars and magazines to put together a collage. Even I can staple precut letters in place and think of interesting things to do with fabric. And I can certainly throw out last year's art projects, straighten shelves, and try a new arrangement for desks. When students walk in on the first day, I want the classroom to look fresh, uncluttered, inviting. I want students to be intrigued by bulletin boards hinting at subjects we'll study during the coming year. Just as important, I want them to know I care enough about their education to have invested a fraction of my summer in getting the room ready for them.

After all, most public-school teachers devote whole days to making their classrooms look welcoming. If our classrooms look tired and shabby by comparison, our students have yet another reason to conclude religious school doesn't really matter. I take ridiculous pride

in remembering the time one of my daughters brought a Christian friend to services and took her into my classroom to see the bulletin boards. "Wow," the friend said, wide eyed, "this looks like *real* school." That's the reaction I want from my students on the first day.

But I always leave one bulletin board empty so students can invest something of themselves in the classroom on that same first day. Books and websites on Jewish education offer many ideas for bulletin boards students can create. Maybe you'll call parents in advance, asking that students come to the first class with photographs of themselves and index cards inscribed with their Hebrew names; maybe you'll invite students to make collages about favorite holidays or Torah stories.

My favorite approach is to cover my desk with objects representing various holidays—a shofar, a menorah, a gragger. As students identify the objects, we take photographs. Soon, the bulletin board labeled "Our Year" is circled with colorful photographs—Rachel holding a jar of honey and biting into an apple, Ben and Erika dangling carrots and broccoli over Jacob's head to form a human sukkah, Jessica grinning as she clutches an oversize tree branch and a Jewish National Fund blue box. When students leave at the end of the day, they've taken the first step toward making the classroom their own.

And that's what we want our classrooms to be—safe, sheltering places, rich in symbols of our heritage and of the harvest the coming year will bring, places that bring together fruits that grow rooted in the earth and dreams that reach the heavens. As teachers, we build the frame for this special sukkah, using our knowledge, experience, and hopes to create an atmosphere that entices students to learn. Our students bring to that framework their questions, energy, and insights. Together, we make something beautiful.

Simḥat Torah: Ending, Beginning, Rejoicing

If any holiday can be singled out as the one that best defines the Jewish teacher's work and purpose, perhaps it is Simḥat Torah. Its themes and symbols embody, precisely and beautifully, what we do, and why we do it.

Simḥat Torah reminds us to rejoice in our work. The study of Judaism, and the teaching of Judaism, are indeed obligations, but they're ones we embrace lovingly and gratefully. As we dance about the sanctuary, we wait eagerly for the moment when the Torah is passed to us; when we feel that familiar weight in our arms, we know we've been entrusted not with a burden but with a treasure, and our hearts thrill to the honor given us. We rejoice in our turn to lead the congregation in following the Torah; we rejoice equally in the privilege of passing the Torah to the next leader.

When we return to our classrooms in September, we feel that same thrill. Once again, the congregation has entrusted its greatest treasures to us. And despite all the difficulties, all the frustrations, we know our students are indeed treasures, not burdens. In our bitterest moments, we may complain that some parents see us as babysitters, but we never see ourselves that way. We know much more goes on in our classrooms. We know we're holding the Torah up before our students, teaching them to recognize how precious it is, preparing them for the day when they'll take it in their own arms, press it to their own hearts, and lead others in the never-ending renewal of the Jewish people. We are teaching the next teachers. Despite all the difficulties, all the frustrations, we rejoice in this sacred task.

And Simḥat Torah teaches us vital lessons about the nature of our joy. These days, we hear much about the yearning for spirituality, about the need for an emotional dimension to religion. Simḥat Torah reminds us of the true foundation of spirituality. On Simḥat Torah, we dance, yes, and we sing. But we also read. We read a double portion of the Torah, and *that* is the basis for our joy. Simḥat Torah tells us spirituality is grounded in more than a vague desire to feel good or connected; rather, spirituality is grounded in study, in careful attention to the words of our sacred texts.

On Simḥat Torah and in our classrooms, intellect and emotion come together, each fueling and supporting the other. Our study leads us to rejoice; our joy compels us to study. Which is more important—the joy that leads to further study, or the study that leads to greater joy? Simḥat Torah reminds us both are part of an eternal cycle. As teachers, we help that cycle endure.

Simḥat Torah also reminds us that Jewish education never ends—not for our students, not for us. We've heard the speeches at bar and bat mitzvah services and at confirmation ceremonies; we've probably made such speeches ourselves. This is not an end, we say, but a beginning; and when we say this, we speak the truth. The end of each stage in Jewish education is the beginning of the next. What holiday embodies that truth more explicitly than Simḥat Torah? We end the reading of the Torah by retelling the death of our greatest prophet. Then we immediately begin again, with the birth of a fresh, new world. The words of the text and the ritual of the holiday lead us to the same truth—every end is a new beginning.

As Jewish teachers, we are living symbols of that truth. We end one school year only to begin another. Through our example, we prove to our students that Jewish education never ends. Year after year, we return to our classrooms. We return to our people's texts and, with our students, study them once again, knowing that this study can never truly be completed—that each year we will learn something new, teach something new. Each year, we become partners in the process of creating new life. This is our obligation, our sacred privilege, our unending joy.

❧ SUGGESTED RESOURCES ❧

The following list of resources, like the lists at the ends of the chapters to come, is clearly not exhaustive. In each list, my purpose is to describe just a few resources related to the themes of the chapter, to help busy teachers get started if they'd like to explore a topic further. Some of the lists mention books, websites, and other resources that offer teachers specific suggestions about ways of teaching the holidays. Some choices on this list may seem idiosyncratic. I haven't always tried to identify the latest or most authoritative text on a subject; often, I've listed personal favorites I've found especially helpful through the years. I hope that you too will find these sources exciting and worthwhile.

Robert Goodman, *Teaching Jewish Holidays: History, Values, and Activities* (Denver: A.R.E. Publishing, 1997).

> Teachers looking for specific ideas for lessons and activities for teaching the holidays will find this book an invaluable resource. Rabbi Goodman covers both major and minor holidays, suggesting techniques and strategies suitable for various grade levels and for family education. His book also includes background information on each holiday, vocabulary and definitions, related blessings, and a list of books, games, tapes, and other resources.

Lawrence N. Mahrer and Debi Mahrer Rowe, *A Guide to Small Congregation Religious Schools* (New York: UAHC Press, 1996).

> Some sections of this book focus on school administration, but others make excellent reading for all teachers as we prepare ourselves for a new year of religious school. For example, the sections on the goals and aims of Jewish education can help us put the coming year in perspective, and the section on curriculum can guide us as we decide what we hope to accomplish in the months ahead. Other sections, such as those on *tzedakah* and family education, can give us ideas for specific projects.

Michael Strassfeld, *The Jewish Holidays: A Guide and Commentary* (New York: Harper and Row, 1985).

> This is the most fascinating book on the Jewish holidays I've ever read. Throughout the year, we can turn to it for facts and ideas about the holidays to share with students and to deepen our own understanding. At the beginning of the year, reading the chapters on the fall holidays can help us focus on the spiritual work that every Jew needs to do during this special season, informing our reflections and preparations as we get ready to return to the classroom.

❖ WEBSITES

As we search for ways to make the coming year even better than the last, we'll find websites a rich and stimulating source of ideas. Especially for those who live in small Jewish communities with few resources, the Internet is a treasure that has truly transformed teaching. Of course, it's important to remember that websites sometimes move or disappear, and that therefore some of the addresses listed here and in other chapters may no longer be accurate.

Teachers' organizations such as the National Association of Temple Educators have valuable websites (**www.rj.org/nate**), and many cities have educational resource centers that also publish websites. (My favorite is the site for the Jewish Education Center of Cleveland, **www.jecc.org**. I especially like the Respons Curricula that help us talk to our students about current events. These curricula are issued in an amazingly timely manner and are consistently excellent.) Some Jewish publishers also have sites that can be rich sources of ideas and advice. Behrman House, for example, sponsors the Educators' Lounge (**www.shalomuvrachah.com/ASPForum**) which invites teachers to share lesson plans and teaching techniques, to ask for suggestions or information, and to trade success stories with other teachers using the same books and materials.

More specialized websites are listed in the chapters that follow. You may also want to spend some time exploring some of the general sites that provide links to hundreds of Jewish resources on the Internet. Here are a few to get you started.

Jewish Community Online | www.jewish.com
Judaism and Jewish Resources | www.shamash.org/trb/judaism
Maven: The Jewish Portal | www.maven.co.il
Judaism 101 | www.jewfaq.org

2. Ḥanukkah

BUILDING JEWISH IDENTITY

It requires religious courage to belong to a minority such as Judaism always has been and always will be. . . . It requires ethical courage to be a Jew when all worldly comforts, honors, and prizes lure him to the other side, and often the Jew has to fight the battle between ideas and interests, between belief and disbelief.

—Leo Baeck, *The Essence of Judaism*

More than two thousand years separate our world from the world of the Maccabees. In many ways, those two worlds have little in common. The Jews of that time lived under a brutal tyranny, forbidden on pain of death to practice their religion, beset by decrees and threats that tried to force them to conform to the ways of their oppressors. We live in a democratic republic, our religious freedom guaranteed by our country's most fundamental laws, our way of life protected by a society that prizes tolerance and individuality as essential virtues. Even so, we may sometimes feel a kinship with the Jews of Judah Maccabee's time.

Like them, we live in a culture that makes abandoning Judaism much easier than remaining faithful. No one stands over us with a sword, compelling us to bow before an idol. Yet the pressures are there, undeniably, tempting us to give up the struggle, to worship at alien altars, to accept the ways of the dominant group. Our students, we can be sure, feel these pressures at least as much as we do—pressures exerted by other religions, by pervasive materialism, and by a popular culture that too often celebrates irreverence, selfishness, and vulgarity. As Jewish teachers, we are charged with the task of helping our students find the courage to resist all such pressures, of helping them build Jewish identities so strong that they can withstand all temptations.

We can see ourselves as continuing the work of Mattathias, the priest forced to become a warrior. Every time we step into our classrooms, we can hear ourselves echoing his cry: "Whoever is for *Adonai* our God, follow me!" But if our work is in some ways far easier than Mattathias's, it is in other ways even more difficult and delicate. We cannot tell our students to strike down the forces that could undermine their Judaism; instead, we must teach them to understand those forces and in some cases even to respect them. We cannot lead our students off into the hills; instead, we must teach them how to live in the midst of temptations. Mattathias protected his soldiers' bodies with armor; we must help our students develop spirits that will shield them not only from external dangers but also from inner weakness and confusion.

And we must remember that there are two Ḥanukkah miracles. One is the miracle of resistance; the other is the miracle of rededication. If the Maccabees had defeated Antiochus and rested content, Judaism might have been lost. But they also returned to the Temple, restored its order and splendor, and relit the eternal light. It took both miracles to ensure Judaism's survival. When we help our students build strong Jewish identities, teaching them to stand firm against the negative forces around them is only half the battle. We must also help them build a positive loyalty to Judaism, by helping them understand and feel the worth and beauty of their Jewish heritage. Only then will they know why the battle matters.

Acknowledging Outside Pressures

As citizens of a modern democracy, we want our students to be open and tolerant. We want them to understand their neighbors' religions, to enjoy the rich variety of traditions they encounter. We do not scold them for thrilling to an excellent performance of Handel's *Messiah*, nor do we teach them to regard Ramadan with horror or to sneer at the evolving observance of Kwanzaa. Often, our curriculum includes units about other religions; always, in such units, respect is a primary objective. We want our students to value diversity, to appreciate other people's beliefs and traditions, and to participate in appropriate ways.

But *only* in appropriate ways—that's the catch. As teachers, we want to be open and tolerant ourselves, and we certainly don't want to teach students to fear everything that's different. But we can see that sometimes other people's ways are a threat to our students. Sometimes, the threat is ugly, perhaps violent. A high school student tells us he found a swastika scrawled on his locker at school; an elementary school student tearfully says two kids at her bus stop shoved her, spit in her hair, and called her a dirty Jew. Sometimes, the threat is peaceful, even friendly. Missionaries waiting across from the public school press green-covered copies of the New Testament into our students' hands; a best friend urges a Jewish student to come to a church retreat and open his heart to Jesus. Often, the threat is so subtle it hardly seems a threat at all. A Girl Scout leader decides her troop will do a good deed by serenading retirement-home residents with "Silent Night"; a first-grade teacher eager to keep students interested finds ways to weave Santa Claus and Christmas trees into every math lesson, every art project, every story hour.

We can't control the experiences students have outside our classrooms, but we can and must listen to what students tell us about those experiences and help them find ways to respond. Otherwise, our students may start to feel that Judaism is an unwelcome burden, forcing them to choose between feeling left out when they don't participate in their friends' activities and feeling guilty when they do. They may feel uneasy in their schools and on their playgrounds, and wonder what it is about Judaism that makes people so hateful toward us. Some students may accept invitations to retreats and come to class with challenging questions; some may even tell us that they don't want to come to our classes at all anymore or that they wish they could go to church rather than to synagogue.

It's not hard to see why other religions, particularly Christianity, might have a strong appeal for some students. Christianity offers clear, guaranteed answers to questions about which Judaism can be maddeningly silent or tentative. Students worried about what happens after death will find more comforting answers at most churches than they will at most synagogues. And Christianity offers them a god with a face, a family, a stirring personal history, and a tragic death. It's far easier to identify with such a figure than it is to feel close to a God who will not reveal a face or even state a definite, unambiguous name. Christianity keeps some of the most attractive elements of Judaism—a noble code of ethics, a conviction that each individual life matters, a sense of community. To these, it adds elements that still make the myths of the Greeks and Romans appealing today—miraculous conceptions and births, battles between good and evil supernatural beings, a god who dies only to be reborn. No wonder some students find such stories exciting and sometimes seductive.

On a more superficial level, traditions associated with Christian holidays can also be powerfully appealing, especially to younger students. My husband and I will never forget the day one of our daughters came home from her supposedly secular preschool, clutching the latest batch of red-and-green art projects, and glumly said, "I wish I could be a Christian, so *I* could have Santa Claus." A jolly, grandfatherly man who drives a team of flying reindeer and slides down your chimney late at night to leave you a pile of presents—what figure could be more perfectly designed to appeal to a child's imagination and desires? It's hard to think of one, unless it might be a magic bunny that hops up your driveway before dawn one spring Sunday and leaves a basket of candy on your doorstep.

Of course, we Jews have beautiful holiday customs of our own. To a child, however, even the most elegant *ḥanukkiyah* may seem unimpressive next to a towering tree hung with sparkling lights and ornaments, with tinsel and angels and stars; and searching for a half piece of matzah hidden in the living room may seem tame compared to hunting for dozens of colorful eggs scattered throughout the house and garden. When almost every store at the mall has mangers or reindeer in its windows, when almost every television show has a heart-warming Christmas episode, when almost every public school has a December concert heavily weighted with Christmas songs—can we be surprised if our students feel deprived? We're up against stiff competition—we might as well admit it.

Sometimes that competition, and the challenge, will be rooted within a student's own family. These days, most classes include students from mixed marriages; one year, I had a class in which every single student had one Jewish parent and one Christian parent. In most of those families, both parents were firmly committed to raising their children as Jews; in some, however, there were tensions, uncertainties, mixtures of customs. How do we talk to students from such families about Jesus, about Santa Claus, about whether Christmas trees belong in Jewish homes? Even some homes with two Jewish parents may have Christmas trees. Over the years, several Jewish parents have told me they put up Christmas trees not because they have Christian spouses, but simply because they don't want their children to feel left out. After all, Christmas trees are just part of secular American culture, so where's the harm?

Just part of secular American culture—if Mattathias were around today, maybe he would decide secular American culture was the first thing he'd have to strike down. In some ways, the most potent influences pulling students away from Judaism are not other religions, but the countless secular forces that encourage our children to think only of themselves, to indulge every desire, and to see every authority figure as oppressive and dumb.

We don't have to be enemies of popular culture to feel this way. I enjoy many movies and television shows, I find many comedians hilarious, and I love rock 'n' roll. But it disturbs me when students come to class wearing T-shirts emblazoned with crude slogans. It bothers me to see how caught up students get in talk about clothes and video games, how unreserved their enthusiasm can be for reality shows that glorify sex and greed or movies that glorify violence. And it saddens me when parents take children out of class early so they can get to their soccer games. At such times, I can't help thinking again about Maccabeean days, about the gymnasiums that tempted too many Jews away from the houses of study, about the Hellenistic obsession with physical beauty and prowess that too often corroded the traditional Jewish devotion to matters of the spirit.

And it can be so hard to get these students to stop being cool. Many seem to come to class determined to be bored by everything and impressed by nothing. And why not? Isn't that the posture adopted by so many of their heroes—the above-it-all, easily cynical young person who sees through every pretension and always has a sarcastic comeback ready? It isn't easy to teach a lesson on the fifth commandment to students who have seen scores of movies portraying parents as at best well intentioned but insensitive, at worst abusive and stupid. It isn't easy to convince students of the need for self-discipline after they've been inundated by commercials telling them to just do it, or of the need for study when so much music and television panders to them by assuring them they already know everything worth knowing.

⁞ *Helping Our Students Become Modern Maccabees*

At times, we may find ourselves envying the Maccabees; at times, charging a squad of soldiers perched atop a battle elephant may seem simpler than combating the many forces, both overt and subtle, confronting today's Jewish educator. How do we help our students develop strong Jewish identities despite all the temptations, all the undermining influences? What weapons can we use, and where do we begin?

We begin, I think, by giving students opportunities to talk about the conflicts they face, strategies for handling those conflicts, and information they can use to defend their decisions. We can also offer support to our students' families, treating all with respect without compromising our roles as Jewish educators; and we can find ways to encourage families to have positive Jewish experiences together. We can work to increase our students' sense of belonging to the Jewish community and to feel strengthened by the support that community offers. We can make special efforts to inform ourselves about the popular culture that can influence our students so profoundly and talk to our students openly about what's good and what's bad about that culture. And always, in every class, we can make sure our words and actions provide our students with a model of someone whose life is shaped by Jewish principles. Always, we can try to make ourselves examples they will want to follow.

Meeting the Challenge of Other Religions

Growing up in a country where Jews form a tiny minority, all of our students have experienced conflicts with Christian culture, and almost all are eager to talk about them. I've often been amazed by just how eager they are. Even in April, if I merely mention the word "Christmas," the stories start pouring out. Students want to talk about the time when they didn't know what to do when the chorus director at public school offered them solos in "Unto Us a Child Is Born"; they want to know whether they should feel guilty about going to a friend's house for dinner and then helping decorate the Christmas tree. And they tell other stories—stories about how weird they felt when they were the only ones who wouldn't eat pepperoni pizza at a sleepover, how mad they felt when the health teacher told them to memorize the Golden Rule for the first quiz, and how scared they felt when friends said that anybody who doesn't believe in Jesus is headed for hell.

When my students tell such stories, I listen closely and sympathetically. Usually, I keep my judgments to myself. I may praise the student who turned down the solo at the Christmas concert, but I don't condemn the student who accepted. Instead, I'll say, "That must have been a tough decision"—and I'll mean it. These are tough decisions, and difficult situations, and our students need our support. We won't get anywhere if they're so afraid of being criticized that they stop telling their stories. And telling their stories is a crucial first step.

We can then look for ways to help our students to take the next step, to help them articulate the challenges implicit in their stories and decide how these challenges can be faced. Especially in larger classes, it may help to break into small groups and ask students to brainstorm about ways to handle the Christmas concert, the sleepover, the health class. Role playing can be useful, too. If your students are anything like mine, they'll jump at any chance to indulge in informal dramatics, and you won't have any trouble finding stars to role-play how to respond to missionaries or what to say to the friend who invites a Jewish student to a church retreat.

These role-plays can be hilarious—with middle school students, try assigning the class clown the role of Bible-thumping missionary—but they serve a serious purpose. In a safe, accepting place, students get a chance to practice asserting their Judaism. They get a taste of how it feels to stay strong, and they enjoy their classmates' applause when they find tactful but effective ways of just saying no. Several years ago, a role-play in my middle school class evolved into a full-fledged play presented at our school's Ḥanukkah assembly, comparing the emotions of a modern teenager feeling left out in December with those of a long-ago teenager struggling to find the spirit to resist Antiochus. Hollywood would not have been impressed by the production values—we just rolled a portable blackboard across the stage to signal shifts between scenes in Judea and scenes in South Dakota—but the play was sweet and funny; it gave my students a way to express what they were feeling, and I think it gave the entire school a lift.

It's also important to give our students some solid information. With younger students, it may be best to keep that information simple. They need to know that it's all right to just say, "No, thanks," and then walk away from missionaries, or to tell friends, "I don't do that because I'm Jewish." Older students may also find that simply walking away from missionaries is usually the best approach. For other situations, older students often want more—arguments they can use when their friends challenge their beliefs, assurances that they're on solid ground when they don't go along with some public school activities. How do they answer a friend who asks them if Judaism regards Jesus as a prophet or tells them the Jewish Bible contains dozens of passages foretelling events in Jesus' life? Students who have been told the United States is a Christian country need to know that the unamended Constitution refers to religion just once, in Article VI, to say that no religious tests shall be required for "any Office or public trust"; they may also be encouraged by studying such documents as George Washington's 1790 letter to the Newport, Rhode Island, Jewish congregation. The list of additional readings corresponding to this chapter describes some books that can help us find the information our students need and get lively, productive discussions going.

It can also help to invite expert guests to the classroom. The rabbi is a natural choice to talk about Judaism's view of Jesus, Jewish interpretations of *Tanach* passages that may seem to refer to Jesus, and Jewish teachings about the Messiah. Some students' parents may be lawyers, political science professors, or public school teachers who have special knowledge and insights to share; it's almost always a thrill for students when their parents come to class as expert guests. A few years ago, our religious school and the adult education committee sponsored a joint program inviting both students and parents to a discussion of holiday conflicts in the public schools. Several members of the congregation had special expertise that helped make the session informative, and families had a chance to talk about their experiences and emotions. These sorts of family education events are easy to arrange, and they give students and parents valuable opportunities to come together to discuss the dilemmas they face.

Other sorts of family education events can be valuable, too. To encourage attendance at such events, students can make invitations and mail them home to their parents. Even parents in the habit of tossing aside photocopied announcements will probably be charmed and intrigued when they receive colorful, personal petitions created by their own children. Family education events need not be elaborate. One year, our religious school organized a simple but enjoyable session for Ḥanukkah. Groups of students and parents circulated from station to station, making latkes, decorating dreidels, learning songs, playing games testing their knowledge about the holiday, and working on puzzles and mazes we got from some of the many Ḥanukkah sites on the Internet. The morning gave families a chance to have fun learning about Ḥanukkah customs together. Maybe it encouraged some families to try these customs at home, too; maybe it convinced some that they don't need to put up trees to enjoy the season.

What do we say about families who *do* put up trees in their homes? Some religious schools have policies about such issues; it's important for teachers to be informed about these policies and to have opportunities to discuss them at faculty meetings. If you're unsure of your school's policies, check with the rabbi or the religious school director. My own position is that it isn't our job to criticize our students' families. Families have a tough enough time holding together these days; if we encourage students to go home and confront their parents about not being Jewish enough, we're not helping. But it *is* our job to teach our students about Judaism.

If students say they have Christmas trees in their living rooms, we don't have to condemn their parents. Instead, we can simply acknowledge the obvious fact that different families make different choices. Then, we can discuss the reasons other families have for making other sorts of choices. Even when there's not much chance of influencing the decisions our students' parents make, we can certainly hope to have a strong influence on the choices our own students make when they become parents themselves and establish their own Jewish homes. If younger students ask if Santa Claus is real, we can say no, explaining that making believe about Santa Claus is a game some parents play with their children and adding that it wouldn't be kind to spoil other children's fun by revealing their parents' secrets. But we can say, firmly, that Jewish children have a right to know the truth. And if older students say parents have told them that a person can believe in Jesus and still be Jewish, I think we have a right to explain, gently but clearly, why that just isn't so.

From time to time, parents may grumble when we give such answers, but I've never yet had one get deeply upset. Almost all parents who send their children to Jewish schools understand that Jewish teachers will present and defend Jewish ideas. As long as we treat other ideas with respect—as long as we don't make fun of Christianity, or encourage students to snicker at anyone who thinks Jesus could be the son of God—almost all parents will acknowledge our right to teach Judaism.

One important part of teaching Judaism, and of building Jewish identity, is helping our students develop a sense of community. Our students' Jewish communities can begin in our own classrooms. To encourage students to see each other as friends and as part of a supportive Jewish network, we can take simple steps such as putting together a list of students' telephone numbers and e-mail addresses, giving all students copies of the list, and encouraging them to keep in touch between classes. We can design homework assignments that reward students who call or e-mail one another to share information or check answers; we can set up "Shabbat Shalom" chains to draw students into the fun and warmth of exchanging greetings on Friday afternoons. To expand the community beyond a single classroom, we can work with other teachers to bring our students together. For example, older students might visit younger students' classrooms to read stories out loud or serve as Hebrew tutors; students from several classes might work together to present assemblies or carry out *tikun olam* projects. In our congregation, students in the confirmation class sometimes serve as substitutes, prepare a lesson for a younger class, or take responsibility for one activity at a family education event.

To further enlarge our students' sense of Jewish community, we can help them develop stronger ties with other members of the congregation, and with the congregation as a whole. Many congregants whose own children are grown take a lively interest in the religious school and relish opportunities to become involved. We can invite such congregants to our classes to describe holiday customs they enjoyed when they were young, to teach students how to make latkes or other traditional foods, or to bring a history lesson to life by talking about how they celebrated the founding of the state of Israel. Every time we bring such a congregant into our classrooms, we give our students another face to recognize the next time they go to services, another reason to feel connected to their Jewish community.

By providing students with opportunities to serve the community, we further strengthen their sense of belonging. Even the youngest students can serve by making decorations for a congregational dinner or holiday celebration or by making cards for congregants in nursing homes; some congregations allow older students to serve on committees, to attend board meetings, or to assume responsibilities such as checking coats at fund-raising events. Quick calls to board officers or committee chairs will probably yield many more ideas about ways of getting students involved in the life of the congregation.

Other sorts of activities make students more aware of the national and international Jewish communities to which they belong. We can use personal or professional contacts to help our students find Jewish pen pals in other cities or in Israel; e-mail makes keeping in touch with such pen pals remarkably easy. If we like, we can give students some class time to send messages to their pen pals or else set aside a few minutes at the beginning of each class to let students share messages they've received during the week. We can also take some time to discuss current events, to keep students informed about news stories of interest to Jews around the world. Another approach is to establish a "Jews in the News" bulletin board and encourage students to bring in any articles they find about members of the congregation, prominent Jews in their city or state, or Jewish leaders in Israel or other countries. Any activity that increases students' sense of being connected to the larger Jewish community affirms their sense of Jewish identity, thereby strengthening their ability to withstand outside pressures.

Responding to Popular Culture

Sometimes, confronting outside pressures directly can be an essential part of our effort to build Jewish identity and encourage students to make Jewish choices. I don't think we can afford to ignore our students' references to the music they listen to, the movies and television shows they watch, or the way they spend their free time; and I don't think it's enough to respond with such remarks as "I don't know why you waste your time with that stuff." Instead, we can take our students' enthusiasms seriously, learn more about them if necessary, and discuss them honestly.

When our students come to class praising shows or movies or songs that sound questionable, we can read some reviews—or, if possible, watch the movie or an episode or two of the show, or borrow a CD and listen to some songs. Watching even a single episode of a television show often gives us enough information to respond intelligently to students' comments and to ask challenging questions, to devote a little class time to a discussion if we judge it worthwhile. We can talk about the actions, values, and goals of the people on the show, then contrast them with the behaviors and ethics Judaism sees as truly admirable. We can also discuss why such shows are popular and examine how the media sometimes appeal to what is lowest in us rather than to what is best. At least some students will probably agree—perhaps reluctantly—that the shows don't promote good values. They may still assert that the shows are fun; chances are, they'll continue to watch. But such discussions can at least make students more aware of a show's shortcomings and more on guard against the influences it might be having. This sort of approach can work equally well with popular movies and songs.

Sometimes, we may discover that the show (or movie, or song) isn't as bad as we feared; sometimes, we may find ways to use short clips from television shows or lyrics from popular songs in class. We can encourage our students to watch and listen critically, noting when one character performs a mitzvah and another misses a chance to do so, or when one song expresses a worthwhile idea and another falls short. We then can make it clear that Judaism has much more to teach us about the subject. In this way, we can help our students to distinguish between what's better and what's worse in popular culture, and to develop the habit of evaluating everything in the context of Jewish ideas.

We don't, of course, want to make popular culture a central or frequent part of our classes. Nor do we ever want to create the impression that watching a television show or listening to a popular song can take the place of studying a Jewish text, no matter how meaningful our students might declare the show or the lyrics to be. But we don't have to condemn everything. We shouldn't disparage shows we haven't seen or songs we haven't heard, no matter how tempted we might be. We can take the time to inform ourselves, or we can refrain from commenting altogether. Otherwise, our students may decide we're like the stereotypical adults who populate young people's movies—the stodgy, ignorant teachers and parents who hate everything youthful and new because they just don't understand. We don't want our students to see us that way—we want them to see us as open minded, fair, and wise.

It's all right if they see us as strict. We can let our students know that there are certain words they may not use in religious school, certain kinds of jokes they may not tell. We can make it clear that we won't be moved by protests that students hear those words on television, or by assertions that their public school teachers don't care when they make those jokes. This, we can tell our students, is religious school; here, different standards apply. We don't worry about being cool here; here, we try to be holy. This is the place where we take refuge from the coarseness and cynicism that pervade so much of modern life. Here, we work at becoming better Jews, better people.

Our students may sometimes see us as old fashioned, may sometimes find our seriousness about Judaism a little weird. That's fine. We're not trying to compete with Howard Stern. We're trying, instead, to set an example as a kind of adult they won't see in many movies—one whose life is shaped by Judaism and devoted to study, who believes that ideas matter, and who is convinced that our religion offers us ideas far more valid and exciting than any we'll find anywhere else. True, our students aren't likely to immediately, consciously accept us as role models. But the strength of our example can be one of the most potent forces influencing students as they find their own paths to Jewish adulthood, a force that will stay with them long after many other influences fade.

Another Ḥanukkah Lesson

And we can have faith that we can, in fact, wage a successful battle against those influences. Among other things, Ḥanukkah teaches us that Judaism can prevail against frightening odds. At times we may feel discouraged when we think of all the forces ranged against our students; Mattathias must have felt discouraged, too, when he saw the vast troops of well-armed Syrian soldiers ranged against his small band of farmers with makeshift weapons. But he knew he was fighting for something far more powerful than anything the Syrians possessed. He did not give up.

Neither do we. We don't relax our vigilance, any more than the Maccabees relaxed theirs. It takes our best efforts to protect our students against the temptations that could weaken their ties to Judaism, to arm them with knowledge, to give them the spirit to grow ever closer to their religion and their people. To sustain ourselves, we remember that Judaism is truer and more beautiful than any of the forces that oppose it. And we watch for small victories: the student who drops out of chorus because she no longer feels right about singing Christmas songs, the student who starts wearing a Star of David pin to public school as a quiet assertion of identity, the day one student reminds another not to use crude language in religious school.

These victories will come—we can be sure of that. My husband and I panicked when our preschool daughter declared she wanted to be a Christian so she could have Santa Claus. By the time she reached kindergarten, she felt smug about knowing Santa Claus wasn't real; by first grade, she was embarrassing us in supermarkets by indignantly cutting off cashiers foolish enough to wish her a merry Christmas— "We don't celebrate Christmas! We celebrate Ḥanukkah! We're Jews!" Now, after majoring in Jewish studies in college, she's spending a year in Jerusalem, studying at a women's yeshiva.

So our panic was premature. It wasn't useless, though, not if it made us work harder at strengthening her Jewish identity. As teachers, we don't have to panic, but we do have to work. We can feel encouraged by the final part of the Ḥanukkah story, when the Jews regained the Temple and poured their one pitiful flask of oil into the eternal light. Perhaps they felt discouraged then—who could have blamed them? But the light burned on.

We relive that drama every year when we light the menorah. On the first night, the light may seem feeble—two small flames, separated by empty space, barely softening the darkness. By the last night, we have a whole row of flames, warm and bright, illuminating the night with a steady, united brilliance that cannot be denied.

As Jewish teachers, we kindle one small light at a time. We know that the light will not kindle itself—we must provide the spark. It takes all our diligence, all our care, all our wisdom, all our love. But this is a sacred light. If we keep rekindling it, year after year, it will endure. It will prevail against the darkness, and grow, and sustain us all.

⬛✳ SUGGESTED RESOURCES ◀⬛

Burton I. Cohen, *Case Studies in Jewish School Management:*
Applying Educational Theory to School Practice
(West Orange, NJ: Behrman House, 1992).

> Parts of this book will be most useful to school administrators and board members, but classroom teachers will also benefit from reading these in-depth portraits of various kinds of religious schools. The sections most relevant to the themes of this chapter focus on the relationship between the school and the community and on ways of building Jewish identity. For example, in Chapter 1, the section called "The Need for an Articulated Educational Philosophy" discusses ways of helping students develop a sense of Jewish identity by involving them in the life of the synagogue and of the Jewish community; Chapter 6 includes a section on "Developing a Jewish Identity Curriculum." Other chapters also contain many insights we can use as we work to increase students' pride in their heritage.

Michael J. Cook, *Missionary Impossible*
(New York: UAHC Press/Jewish Institute of Religion, 1998).

> Dr. Cook and a number of his rabbinic students at Hebrew Union College put together this video and curriculum guide to offer teachers and students strategies for responding to Jews for Jesus and other missionary groups. The video features four skits, acted out by the rabbinic students, as well as college and high school students, showing "genuine situations where Jewish youth may encounter missionaries, how they might respond, and then how they should respond." The curriculum guide suggests ways of using the video in class and also contains background information on topics such as freedom of religion and differences between Judaism and Christianity.

Andrea King, *If I'm Jewish and You're Christian, What Are the Kids?*
(New York: UAHC Press, 1993).

This book explores the challenges interfaith families face at various times in their lives together—before children are born, as the children grow up, after the children leave home. It also explores special topics such as relationships with grandparents. Teachers who read this book will get a richer sense of the experiences of interfaith families. It can help us see past the stereotyped notions that any Jew who marries a gentile can't care much about Judaism, and that Christian parents are bound to be either hostile or indifferent about their children's Jewish education. The author herself provides us with a moving example of a Christian parent firmly committed to working hard to see that her children are raised and educated as Jews.

Harold S. Kushner, *When Children Ask About God*
(New York: Schocken, 1971).

This book is a wonderful resource for teachers seeking ways to respond to the hard questions our students often ask us about a wide range of issues. Many sections of the book are relevant to issues raised in this chapter: What do we say to students who ask us what God looks like, or what happens after death, or whether Judaism promises us salvation? Rabbi Kushner explores such questions with great honesty and depth, helping us find answers young people can understand without denying the complexity of Judaism's teachings or the variety of Jewish opinions on such subjects. It's interesting to compare this book with another excellent resource, David J. Wolpe's *Teaching Your Children About God: A Modern Jewish Approach* (New York: HarperCollins, 1995). Rabbi Wolpe considers many of the same questions as Rabbi Kushner but sometimes offers very different answers—further proof that Judaism embraces many ideas and beliefs, and that easy, undisputed answers can be hard to find.

Samuel Levine, *You Take Jesus, I'll Take God: How to Refute Christian Missionaries* (Los Angeles: Hamorah Press, 1980).

This book has an in-your-face title and an in-your-face attitude, and some people don't like it for just that reason. I like it a lot. The author analyzes the motives and tactics of Christian missionaries and provides us with questions we can use to challenge their assumptions. As teachers, we may find the most useful section to be the one commenting on the *Tanach* passages missionaries often use to argue that Jesus was the Messiah. In my opinion, Levine does a fine job of tearing these arguments apart, showing how the passages have to be yanked out of context and twisted past recognition to support the interpretations sometimes imposed upon them. It's helpful to become familiar with this section, and to review it from time to time, so we'll know how to respond when students come to us confused by things they've heard from missionaries and friends; with older students, we may choose to devote a class or two to discussing the passages in question.

WEBSITE

Jews for Judaism | www.jewsforjudaism.org

Jews for Judaism describes itself as "the Jewish community's leading response to the multi-million dollar efforts of deceptive missionary and cult groups that target Jews for conversion." The organization has offices in several United States cities and also in several other countries. The website offers educators a number of resources, including essays on topics related to missionary groups, a newsletter, information about speakers and publications, and links to other sites.

3. Tu B'Shevat

PLANTING, NURTURING, BLOSSOMING

*"If you should happen to have a sapling
in your hand when they tell you the
Messiah has arrived, first finish planting.
Then, go out and greet the Messiah."*

—Yochanan ben Zakkai,
Avot de-Rabbi Natan, 31b

Jewish teachers often quote Yochanan ben Zakkai's saying when Tu B'Shevat draws near. His words, we tell our students, point to the enormous importance of trees. Then we pass out the Jewish National Fund blue boxes and talk about the role planting trees has played in reclaiming the land of Israel. Later, among ourselves, we may give the saying a more cynical interpretation, joking about the widespread Jewish skepticism about whether the Messiah will ever come.

Perhaps a combination of these two interpretations is most helpful to us as teachers. The hope for the coming of the Messiah or a Messianic age is a powerful theme in Judaism. For centuries, Jews have waited for a great change that will forever establish universal peace, justice, and truth; but while we're waiting, we don't hold our breath. Instead, we tend steadily to the business of this world. We keep planting trees.

Similarly, as teachers, we may yearn for the one decisive breakthrough that will make all the difference in our students' lives. Late at night, while we're flipping channels on the television, we may catch a few moments of a revival meeting, we may see the people rushing forward to proclaim they've been saved, and we may wish our words could have that kind of impact. But although such fantasies may make us smile wistfully as we drift into sleep, they don't keep us lying awake all night. The revival meeting is not a model for Jewish education. As nice as sudden, complete moments of transformation would be, we know education seldom happens that way. Usually, it's a long, slow process, more akin to planting and nurturing trees than to instantly infusing people with inspiration. And just as a farmer knows a forest will never come to be unless each sapling receives the care it needs, we know a child becomes educated only when each class is carefully planned and presented.

It's instructive to remember that Yochanan ben Zakkai was, above all, a teacher. On the most famous night of his life, when Jerusalem was about to fall and Judaism itself faced extinction, he risked death by pretending to die. He had his students carry him outside the city in a coffin, he confronted the Roman general, and he delivered his startling prophecy, declaring that the general would soon be named emperor of Rome—his shrewd prophecy, carefully grounded in fact. And when the prophecy proved accurate and the general offered him a reward, ben Zakkai asked for permission to found a school. How fearful about Judaism's future ben Zakkai must have felt that night; how natural it would have been for him to yearn for the miraculous arrival of the Messiah to save his city and his religion. Sadly, the Messiah did not come, and Jerusalem, for cruelly long centuries, was lost. But the sages who taught at ben Zakkai's school kept Judaism alive. Our religion, and our people, survived devastating loss and exile because Jewish education went on in its gradual but unyielding way, lesson after patient lesson, class after careful class.

☙ *The Individual Class Session: A Living Structure*

The farmer planting saplings may dream of a forest but meanwhile makes sure each particular sapling gets the care it needs. In our work, we are guided by our goals for the year and our understanding of the curriculum as a whole, but meanwhile we pay careful attention to each individual class and to each student within it. Whether we're teaching one subject or many, whether we have one hour with our students, two hours, or even three, we want each class session to be satisfying, unified, and complete.

It's good if each session has a unifying theme or idea, so that students see it as more than a succession of unrelated tasks. If we're teaching just one subject, finding such a theme or idea can be relatively easy. If we're with our students for two or three hours and need to cover a range of subjects—say, Hebrew and history and ethics and sacred texts—making the class seem unified and whole can be much more challenging.

Sometimes, if the curriculum leaves us a great deal of freedom, careful planning at the beginning of the year can help us find unifying themes for our classes. We might decide, for example, to build each class around the weekly Torah portion, or around one particular mitzvah. We can then teach our students related Hebrew prayers and vocabulary, discuss relevant ethical principles, and bring up Jewish heroes or *Tanach* stories that illustrate these principles. Perhaps we'll provide historical background or draw connections with holidays. Some textbooks are designed to support such an approach; if we choose our own textbooks, we can look for those that help us find a unified focus for each class.

Sometimes, however, our textbooks are chosen for us, and we're asked to cover, in each class, a number of apparently unrelated subjects. Even so, we can sometimes find a way to bring at least some of those subjects together. In one class, I needed to discuss the High Holy Days, cover the first chapter in a history text, and review some Hebrew basics; I also wanted to tell my students about a Jewish baseball player who had recently decided not to play in an important game on Yom Kippur and made a public statement about being true to one's roots. Roots provided the central image for the class. I made a large cardboard cutout of a tree and taped it to the blackboard. As we studied the roots of the Jewish people and root letters of Hebrew words, we added words and letters around roots and branches to illustrate principles we discussed; stretching the image a bit, we talked about how our happiness throughout the year can be rooted in our thoughts and actions during the Days of Awe. I think organizing our study around a central image made the class more unified and memorable for the students; it definitely spurred me to find fresh ways of presenting familiar material.

Paying attention to the structure of each class can also help create a sense of unity and purpose. When we teach our students the word *siddur*, we remind them of the role order plays in the Jewish service. It's important, we say, that each service has a definite beginning, middle, and end—that it starts in a way that calls us together and prepares us, that its central prayers follow a familiar and meaningful order, that its conclusion helps us leave the synagogue with renewed insight and determination.

The wisdom embodied in the structure of the service can guide us as we plan each individual class session. Even if we need to cover several subjects in a single lesson, even if we can't always find a unifying idea or image, we still can find ways of helping students to see each class as orderly and purposeful, to realize they aren't simply meandering from topic to topic until the required amount of time has passed.

We can use various approaches here. We can make sure that we always study subjects in a set order, and that our students know this order and understand its logic. Or, before class begins, we can list key words on the board, checking each one off as we come to it. This simple technique helps students see that we have a plan for the class. We may also develop small rituals to mark the beginning, middle, and end of class, to give students the sense that they know what's going on, and that they're moving ahead.

⅄ *Planting a Seed: Opening Class, Engaging Students*

The first time I taught religious school, the kindergartners in my class didn't wait three minutes before letting me know I was doing everything wrong. I'd started class—sensibly enough, I thought—by introducing the first topic I wanted to discuss with them. But these students had already had a week of public school; they knew I'd skipped a step. Before we got to work, they told me, I should assign helpers because that's what their public school teachers did. At first, I shrugged the suggestion off. After all, the class was so small that I could easily handle tasks such as distributing art supplies myself. I didn't need helpers; the whole idea sounded silly. But the students insisted, so I indulged them.

The next week, I came to class with a large poster board chart labeled "Shining Stars" and a stack of Star of David cutouts. The chart listed enough classroom chores to cover all the students, and each star had a student's name on the front and a loop of masking tape on the back. From then on, we began each class by rotating the stars, assigning each student a task for the day. For a while, the ritual still struck me as silly. Most of the chores were blatantly make-work—passing out pencils, leading *Hamotzi* before snack, collecting papers. But the students loved it. Each week, they waited eagerly as I moved their stars to the next slots, and they claimed their responsibilities proudly— "Look! This week, *I* lead the line to children's services!" Before long, I saw how an opening ritual—virtually any opening ritual—can help students make the transition from ordinary activities to study, and can make a class seem coherent and orderly.

Even before class begins, we can start to create an atmosphere for study by getting to our rooms early enough to greet students as they arrive, playing a tape of Jewish music, or writing on the board a question students can answer if they dig out their textbooks and start hunting. I've found posting a question to be a particularly effective technique. Students come to temple joking around, chatting about sports and television. Then they see the question—for example, "Which of our Hebrew vocabulary words ends in a sounded vowel?" Usually, some students keep chatting, but some want to be the first to find the answer. By the time I close the door, several books are open, and several hands are raised. The transition from socializing to studying has begun—painlessly, even playfully.

We might then use some sort of opening ritual to complete the transition, choosing one that suits the nature of our class, the age of our students, and our own strengths as teachers. We can have children sing a song or recite a prayer (perhaps the blessing traditionally said before beginning Torah study). We can ask students to keep homework logs in their notebooks and open class by having those students who completed their assignments reward themselves with stickers. We may invite each student to share something he or she did during the week. We can have a flashcard review of this week's Hebrew vocabulary words, or a quick team game of Concentration using Hebrew letters. With older students, we might open by discussing a passage from the weekly Torah portion or current events of Jewish interest. If a particular session has a central theme, we can begin by introducing it— writing a mystery word on the board and challenging students to define it when discussion makes its meaning clear, holding up an object and asking students to raise their hands when they figure out how it's related to the topics being studied, even tantalizing students by holding up a snack and declaring they can't eat it until they figure out its significance. (Once, the week before Rosh Hashanah, I drove a middle school class nearly insane by withholding a bag of Bugles until one boy finally realized the treats were shaped like shofars.)

Whatever ritual we choose, it will probably work best if it's something that the students enjoy and that helps them focus on the work about to begin. It should also be something we repeat often enough to create a sense of order and expectation. I'll confess I found one of my favorite models of good teaching not in Jewish tradition but on public television's *Mr. Roger's Neighborhood*. Mr. Rogers began each show in exactly the same way: entering his special house, changing from jacket and shoes to sweater and sneakers, singing his welcoming song. Day after day, my daughters were drawn in by this ritual. Whatever they'd been doing before Mr. Rogers began strolling up that path, they put it aside willingly; by the time he was ready to begin his lesson, they were entranced—and so was I. Eagerly, we waited to go wherever he wanted to take us. It was hard for anyone, of any age, to turn away once Mr. Rogers had invited us to learn with him. If we can make the opening moments of our classes half as enticing as the opening moments of his shows, we're on our way.

⅄ *Nurturing: Helping Students Learn Throughout the Class*

If class begins well, we'll have captured our students' attention. Now, we have to hold onto that attention—for one hour, two hours, perhaps three. It's crucial, of course, that the content of the class is excellent. We need to make sure that we've chosen important, compelling material; that we've made sure it's neither so advanced that our students feel overwhelmed nor so elementary that they don't feel challenged; that we ourselves have prepared so thoroughly that we can teach with confidence and provide fascinating insights into the material we discuss. Even when the content of a class is strong, however, we all know how easy it is for students to get distracted, to get tired of concentrating and lapse into lethargic silence, to yield to the temptation to liven things up by misbehaving.

We've all heard of tricks and techniques teachers can use to deal with such problems. Most have some merit, but most have limitations, too. The best approach may be to begin by admitting that holding a child's attention for any length of time is inherently difficult. (For that matter, holding an adult's attention for two or three hours isn't easy, either.) We can begin by making our expectations realistic: No matter how hard we try, no matter how well we do, sometimes our students will lose interest, sometimes they will not respond, sometimes they will act up. So it's important for us to come to class with good-humored determination, knowing that problems are bound to arise, armed with techniques that can help us deal with those problems, resigned to the fact that no technique will work every time. This challenge makes teaching endlessly frustrating but also endlessly stimulating. No formula can do our work for us; no formula can take the place of the individual teacher's ability to stay flexible, stay creative, stay optimistic.

For example, we may have been told that since young people have short attention spans, we have to keep our classes moving at breakneck speed to keep students from getting bored. We may have been told we need to switch constantly from topic to topic and from teaching method to teaching method; one expert once solemnly informed me that since I was teaching middle-school students, I had to introduce a new activity every five minutes. Such experts may point to television as proof that young people stay interested only when each hour is broken into many tiny segments.

Undoubtedly, many students have short attention spans. There's still the question, however, of how much we should cater to those short attention spans, of whether we should make a conscious attempt to lengthen them, of whether our classes should move as quickly as most television shows. People complain that watching television is too passive; perhaps the frantic pace is one reason for the passivity. Things race by so fast that we're lucky if we can absorb a few bits of information—there's no time to reflect, to think of different ways to approach a topic, to disagree, to move to a higher level of understanding. A class that moves that quickly can be exciting in a superficial way, but we don't want our classes to be slick presentations that merely keep students entertained and docile. We want them to be times of coming together to participate, to share, to challenge each other, to think, to learn. That's when classes get truly exciting.

So we needn't make switching topics every few minutes an ironclad rule. Some activities take no longer, but others can't be truly worthwhile if we hurry them that much. A flashcard review of *alef-bet* letters might go very quickly; when we ask students to fit letters together and sound words out, we probably need to relax the pace. When we discuss a Torah passage or ethical principle, we need to slow the pace still more. Sometimes, we can keep classes lively by alternating between fast-paced activities and slow-paced ones—a quick game followed by an intense discussion of a prayer, ten minutes to learn a Hebrew song followed by an art project that gives students time to make careful decisions about how to express their ideas. Always, we can be ready to adjust the pace of class to suit the students' responses. If students get deeply involved in a discussion and want to linger over a topic, we can let them; if they grow restless, we can put a lesson aside sooner than planned, do something else for a while, and return to that lesson later.

It helps to over-prepare a bit, to have one or two sure-to-please activities in reserve in case we need to liven a class up. Almost any sort of game will get a class moving again. For example, we can keep in our desk a box full of slips of paper with clues for Jewish charades or Pictionary, and pull the box out for a ten-minute game if we sense that students are starting to get droopy. (The chapter on Purim contains more suggestions for classroom games.) We can also keep on hand flashcards we can use for quick reviews of Hebrew vocabulary or other material. When I teach *Tanach* stories, I keep two sets of index cards in my desk, with the name of a story or character written on each card. When the class needs a change of pace, I divide the class into two teams, give each team a set of cards, and see which team can put the cards into the proper order first. We can use similar techniques for quick reviews of the order of historical events or of the parts of the Shabbat service. We can also keep an emergency folder stocked with copies of word searches, mazes, rebuses, or other sorts of pencil-and-paper activities. Many workbooks and websites offer such puzzles for students of various ages. Getting pencils into hands and minds focused on a challenging, well-defined task for a few minutes can be an effective way of reviving students' attention and energy.

To avoid having to resort to such emergency measures too often, we can build a variety of approaches into our plans for any class session. Few classes can sustain a discussion for an hour, or listen to a lecture for half that long. To keep things moving, we can combine some activities that involve the whole class, some small-group activities, and some individual work in each session. We can introduce a topic to the full class with a brief presentation, have students break into pairs or small groups to discuss it or find an answer to a question, come back together to compare ideas, then have students work individually on activity sheets or art projects. All that can happen in about half an hour. We can also find other ways to add variety to a class—showing a five-minute clip from a Jewish video, taking students to the library to pick out books, or introducing them to a Jewish website.

Suppose we're planning an introductory lesson on Tu B'Shevat. Before students arrive, we might set up a display of objects such as a bowl of orange sections, a box of dates, a bag of almonds, a bottle of apple juice, a container of cinnamon, a newspaper, a pencil, and so on.

We can then open class by challenging students to figure out what all of these objects have in common. Depending upon the age of the students, it probably won't be long before someone figures out that everything in the display comes from trees. We might then divide the class into small groups and have them brainstorm about why trees are important, then call the groups together to compare their ideas. Perhaps one or two students can serve as class scribes, drawing up a master list of ideas on the board. The next part of the lesson might be a short discussion of Tu B'Shevat. We can include some Hebrew in the lesson. For young students, the blessing said before eating fruit is one natural choice; for older students, more challenging vocabulary related to the holiday or to trees might be appropriate. Students might break into pairs to practice the Hebrew, then come together to say the blessing and enjoy the edible parts of the display. While students are eating, we might play a tape of Tu B'Shevat songs or show *The Blue Box* or another short video available from the Jewish National Fund. Another discussion, this one focusing on why trees are important to Israel, might follow. The lesson might conclude with an art project; perhaps students could make posters encouraging other students to save up to plant trees in Israel, then display the posters in the school's hallways or on a public bulletin board. By using such a variety of techniques, we can keep class lively while still allowing time for slower-paced activities.

During those slower-paced activities, there are other techniques we can use if our students' attention starts to lag. All teachers sometimes have trouble getting discussions going. We introduce a fascinating topic or ask a provocative question, we wait for our students' eager responses—and nothing happens. The students who seemed so spirited when they came into class now stare back at us blankly or, embarrassed, avoid looking at us altogether.

At such times, it's tempting to rephrase the question in a dozen different ways in a desperate attempt to get a response, or to give up and answer it ourselves. Sometimes, though, the best thing we can do is simply to stay quiet for a few moments, simply to wait. When I first started teaching, a fellow graduate student gave me one of the most valuable pieces of advice I've ever received. When you ask a question and no one responds, she said, count to ten—silently, and slowly. You'll be surprised at how often someone speaks up before you finish. When we're in front of a classroom, any silence seems endless. We feel as if no one has said anything for hours, as if the class will wither and die unless we get things going again immediately. Usually, though, the silences are much shorter than they feel; often, the students just need a few seconds to think. If we give them that time, they'll respond, often surprising us with the depth and originality of their comments.

When a silence lasts more than ten seconds, I sometimes ask the question again and tell students to jot their ideas down on paper; then, I ask students to share what they've written. This technique almost always works. Even students who are reluctant to talk in class are usually willing to write their ideas down and then read them out loud when invited to do so. Many students, I think, are grateful for this extra prompting: They have ideas they'd like to share, but they may lack the confidence to speak up, especially when the eager talkers in a class tend to dominate. Even when a discussion is already lively, using this technique can be a good way of drawing out the quieter students.

Taking a few minutes for writing can also be an effective way of ending a discussion. When we finish discussing a *Tanach* story, a holiday, or virtually any other subject, we can ask students to reflect for a moment, write a sentence or two summing up what they see as the most important idea discussed, and then share what they've written with the class. This technique encourages students to think about what they've learned and increases the chances that they'll retain it. It also helps us check up on how well students have understood a lesson, alerting us to points we might need to review.

⚘ Blossoming: Ending Class Effectively

Tu B'Shevat is celebrated at the time when the almond trees in Israel bloom. Although the trees have not yet borne fruit, a blossom is a beautiful thing in itself, and it holds the promise of what is to come. No matter how good a class session is, we'll seldom end with a sense of full completion. If we end with a sense that something has blossomed, or is about to blossom, that's enough.

Just as it's good for a class session to have a definite beginning, it's good if it has a definite ending—and if the ending leaves students eager for the next beginning, so much the better. For years, I was so eager to take full advantage of every bit of class time that I taught halfway through the last minute of each session. Class always ended in confusion as students hurled textbooks into book bags and charged the door, while I desperately scrawled a homework assignment on the board, shouting, "Wait! Don't pack up yet! *Nobody* leaves until *everybody* writes down the assignment! Charlie, that means *you*! Get away from that door!"

Finally, I realized that having the final minutes of class disintegrate into chaos is not an especially effective teaching technique. Finally, I learned another lesson from Mr. Rogers and decided to end class with a calm winding-down period, with a few moments for reflection and preparation. I thought of Mr. Rogers taking off his sneakers and sweater, putting on his shoes and jacket, chatting quietly about what had been learned, singing a song about next time. Nothing I could teach in the last minutes of class could be as effective as giving students a few moments to glance back, shift gears, and look ahead. Now, I keep a careful eye on my watch as the end of class nears, stop when we have at least five minutes left, and try to end the session in an orderly, useful way.

With younger students, singing the same song at the end of every class creates a sense of ritual. A song such as "Shalom Ḥaverim" is simple enough for the youngest students to learn, and the chorus of "*l'hitraot*"— "till we meet again"—leaves everyone looking forward to the next class.

With students of any age, some way of reviewing what's happened during class can help everyone realize something has indeed been accomplished. I like giving my middle school students half-sheets of colored paper headed "Today in religious school, we . . ." As students call out suggestions, I list points on the board, trying to focus on the central themes and most important ideas covered. The students copy the list onto their sheets, which I then staple to any handouts the students have received during class, fervently hoping these materials become the basis of family discussions, perhaps helping to keep learning going during the week.

Whatever other closing rituals we adopt, we may also want to end class by assigning homework. An assignment can be one way to extend learning into the week, especially if it has a hook—a question students should be able to answer when they come back to class, a mysterious word they'll learn to define when they do the reading. With luck, such assignments may pique students' curiosity and make them look forward to the next class, or at least motivate them to do their homework so they can be the first to answer when we ask the hook question or present the mystery word next week.

Religious-school students are notorious for not doing homework, but the majority will generally do most of it most of the time if we keep the assignments reasonably short and find ways of recognizing and rewarding those who do their work. For example, we might allow students who have completed assignments to put stickers on a bulletin board set aside for that purpose, then give the whole class a special snack or other treat when the required number of stickers has been accumulated. Younger students, especially, can get remarkably caught up in the excitement of working toward a make-your-own-sundae or pizza-for-breakfast morning; I've seen them get to class early so that they can count the stickers on the board, and heard them remind each other to do their assignments so that the class can reach its goal more quickly. Some teachers might see such a technique as bribery; I think it's harmless fun. And if it gets students to open their books during the week, that's good enough for me.

The Internet also offers ways to keep students learning and interested after class ends. You can create an email list in your address book and send your students one or two quick messages between classes—a few words about an idea that came to you while doing the reading for class, a comment about something that's happened in Israel, a reminder about a special event at temple, a *Shabbat shalom*. If you subscribe to online Jewish newsletters or weekly Torah commentaries, you might forward these to your students, perhaps challenging them to read the material and find the answer to a question. When holidays approach, you can take advantage of websites that allow you to send free e-cards. All students love receiving these cards, and some love hunting through newsletters and commentaries to find answers to questions. It never works with the whole class—inevitably, some students say their computers are down. But sending an e-mail message is a wonderfully quick, easy way to keep in touch with students between classes. A synagogue website offers another alternative: If you can post messages there, even students who don't own computers can check the site at school.

⅄ A Tu B'Shevat Story: The Old Man and the Carob Tree

Sooner or later, in lessons on Tu B'Shevat, we almost all tell our students the story of a sage named Honi, who comes across an old man planting a carob tree. "When will that tree bear fruit?" Honi asks. "In seventy years," the old man answers. Honi laughs. "Foolish man," he says. "Do you expect to live long enough to eat that fruit?" And the old man replies, "I have often eaten the fruit of carob trees planted by those who came before me. Now, by planting trees for those who come after me, I repay a debt."

As teachers, we may never see the fruit of most of the trees we plant. No matter how carefully we plan, we seldom see tangible results by the time a session ends, or even by the time a year ends. Our students leave us with so much still to learn, often still with attitudes that make us cringe. Even so, like the old man planting the tree, we faithfully plan class after class—placing seeds in the earth, nurturing saplings, knowing we may never see the fruit these fragile young trees will bear but believing nonetheless that the trees will grow, the fruit will come.

Sometimes, if we're lucky, we glimpse that fruit. More than once, I've attended the bar or bat mitzvah service or confirmation ceremony of a student I taught years before and been jolted nearly out of my seat when the student referred in a *d'var Torah* to a discussion we'd had in class long ago. More than once, I've been astonished to hear a student declare he or she decided to make a Jewish hero or heroine we'd studied a model for his or her own life, or adopted a mitzvah we'd discussed as a personal goal. I remembered how bored the student had looked during that long-ago class, and I felt stunned and humbled. Somehow, in ways I couldn't see at the time, those classes had worked.

Several years ago, my husband and I took our daughters to visit the temple where we had been married more than a quarter of a century ago—Temple Beth Am, in Buffalo, New York. On the day we visited, the volunteer working in the office happened to be Mrs. Goldberg, who taught the religious school class I'd attended as a kindergartner. She showed us the new additions to the temple and told stories about classmates I'd lost touch with years ago. She was warm and charming, and we had a lovely time. No wonder I'd always loved religious school, I thought as we drove away. With Mrs. Goldberg as my first teacher, how could I not find it a sheltering, nurturing, fascinating place?

I hope our chance meeting was a good experience for her, too. I hope she found satisfaction in learning that an old student was now a religious school principal, that my husband taught religious school too, that one of our daughters was majoring in Jewish studies at college and the other was eagerly preparing for her bat mitzvah. I hope it was some reward for the many hours she devoted to preparing and teaching classes, and for any headaches I'd caused her. If we hadn't happened to visit the temple on that day, she would never have known about these particular fruits of her labors.

As Jewish educators, we may or may not see the affirmation of our efforts, but we can be sure that affirmation exists. If we tend faithfully to our work, we can be certain our students will live more fully Jewish lives as a result. And we can be sure they'll some day plant seeds of their own—as parents, as congregation members, perhaps as teachers. By teaching, we repay our debts to our own teachers, and we keep planting the seeds that nourish the next generation of teachers and help them keep working—class after careful class, lesson after patient lesson, until the Messiah comes.

✹ SUGGESTED RESOURCES ❧

Merrill Harmin, *Inspiring Active Learning: A Handbook for Teachers* (Alexandria, Va.: Association for Supervision and Curriculum Development, 1994).

> Jewish teachers will be able to adapt many of the ideas in this handbook to meet our needs. The author describes techniques we can use to make each class session a lively, engaging time of learning and mutual respect. For example, she suggests ways of devising homework assignments that help students become more responsible, independent learners.

Rabbi Daniel B. Fink and the Hadassah National Jewish Education Department, *Judaism and Ecology* (New York: Hadassah, 1993).

> This study guide is a valuable resource for teachers seeking ideas for lessons related to Tu B'Shevat. The book offers a historical overview of

environmental problems, explores ideas about ecology reflected in various Jewish texts, and describes "hands-on ecological solutions" that can be undertaken by individuals or groups. Most chapters include thought-provoking quotations from Jewish sources, study questions, and lists of further readings.

Eric Jensen, *Super Teaching* (Del Mar, California: Turning Point for Teachers, 1995).

Jensen discusses a wide range of topics, from ideas about learning styles and multiple intelligences to building good relationships with students and parents. Most relevant to the concerns of this chapter are the sections on lesson planning, presenting skills, successful interactions, and rituals and affirmations. Most of the strategies Jensen describes can be adapted to teach virtually any subject matter and students of virtually any age.

Robert J. Marzano, Jennifer S. Norford, Diane E. Paynter, Debra J. Pickering, and Barbara B. Gaddy, *A Handbook for Classroom Instruction That Works* (Alexandria, Virginia: Association for Supervision and Curriculum Development, 2001).

Based on extensive research and surveys, this book describes a range of "instructional strategies proven to improve student achievement" in K–12 classrooms. Chapters focus on topics such as homework, learning groups, and setting objectives and providing feedback. The book includes many practical suggestions, for example, using graphic organizers.

Mel Silberman, *Active Learning: 101 Strategies to Teach Any Subject* (Boston: Allyn and Bacon, 1996).

Silberman provides an introduction to ideas about active learning, then describes—as his title promises—101 practical techniques teachers can use in the classroom. His short chapters cover topics such as ways to stimulate discussions, ideas for collaborative learning and peer teaching, exercises that help students master new skills, techniques for reviewing material, and strategies for assessment and self-assessment.

4. Purim

TEACHING AS CELEBRATION

A person in a joyful mood can learn more in one hour than a depressed person can learn in many hours.

—Rabbi Chaim Volozhin, *Ruach Chaim*
(commentary on *Pirkei Avot*)

Purim is a joyous holiday, but the Purim story is hardly a lighthearted fable. True, it contains elements of romance and irony: the Cinderella-like girl who becomes queen, the turnaround when Haman thinks he's describing the way he'll be honored but is in fact outlining plans to exalt his enemy. Other elements of the story, however, are harsh, even horrific. The Jews are a vulnerable minority in a foreign land, facing a villain so implacable that he wants to avenge a personal snub by wiping out an entire people. Every Jewish man, woman, and child in Persia faces imminent death; a Jewish girl is so afraid of being executed by her husband that she nearly turns her back on her people; the Jews must fight for survival, and their safety is secured only through the deaths of Haman, his sons, and his followers.

In another religion, Purim might have become a somber commemoration of suffering. Or it might have become an occasion for pure revelry, its dark roots obscured and almost forgotten, like the origins of Halloween. Judaism takes a different approach—a balanced, comprehensive approach. We don't hide the facts of the Purim story. Instead, we remind ourselves of them every year through a public reading of the *Megillah*, and some Jews fast in remembrance of the ordeal the Jews of Persia endured. But the fast is relatively easy— sunrise to sunset rather than twenty-four hours—and the reading becomes a raucous celebration. Then we give ourselves over to games, songs, plays, gift giving, and special foods (and even, for adults, a bit too much alcohol). The poor are also remembered; even when we focus on celebrating our own deliverance, we do not neglect *tzedakah*. The observance of Purim reflects Judaism's balanced, comprehensive view of life, one that encompasses both recognition of life's troubles and affirmation of its joys, both our need for occasional self-indulgence and our enduring obligations to others.

Jewish education can strive for similar balance and comprehensiveness. We've probably all known teachers who always turn down invitations to have their classes put on the Purim play. "We don't have time," they say. "We have too much material to cover." We've also probably all known teachers who have just about given up on covering material, who are so afraid of being boring that they've cut the content of their classes down to practically nothing. Teachers can take extreme approaches to discipline, too, either by being so intent on maintaining order that students grow rebellious, or by being so indulgent that students take control of the classroom.

Thinking about the way Purim is observed can help us find a mean between such extremes. Study is, of course, central to Jewish education, just as reading the *Megillah* is central to Purim observance. Our classes will always include Hebrew drills and history lessons, and students will always need to do some hard work to learn the things informed, committed Jewish adults need to know. But on Purim we learn not only by hearing the story of Esther and Mordecai but also by taking part in celebrations that help us share their feelings of joy, gratitude, and triumph. Similarly, in Jewish education, we needn't feel that any deviation from strict attention to books means abandoning learning. Hard work can be balanced by joyful play, and our classes can be comprehensive enough to include activities that give students a sense of release from routine while still helping them learn about and grow to treasure Judaism.

Keeping the good-humored spirit of Purim in mind also helps us maintain our balance about discipline. We need to keep the focus on work, but we don't want our classrooms dominated by rules and reprimands. Instead, we want them to be relaxed, friendly places where students want to cooperate, want to learn. The lessons we learn by celebrating Purim can help us achieve this goal as well.

✕ The Visual Arts: Expressing Thoughts, Creating Treasures

In November 1995, like countless other Jewish teachers, I asked my students to share their thoughts about a shocking event. Yitzhak Rabin had been assassinated, and I wanted my fifth-graders to have a chance to talk about it. Most spoke up eagerly, asking questions, expressing their confusion and sorrow. Eva said nothing. That wasn't surprising—she was a newcomer in a class of students who had been together for years. Besides, she seemed to be the naturally quiet type. I tried to draw Eva into the discussion but received little response, so I gave up and turned to the students waiting impatiently for another chance to talk.

The next morning, Eva's mother sent me an e-mail message. When Eva came home from religious school, she'd drawn a border of Jewish symbols around a sheet of paper. In the middle she'd written, "Shalom, Mr. Rabin." Her mother was touched; so was I. It reminded me that students have many ways of expressing their thoughts; those who don't take part in discussions aren't necessarily uninterested. It also made me realize it wouldn't have been a waste of classroom time if I'd ended the discussion by passing out paper and markers.

Another incident, a few years later, taught me another lesson about making the visual arts part of Jewish education. I'm a firm believer in having special book bags for religious school—without them, students are likely to scatter textbooks all over the house and car and show up for class unprepared—so I'd made it a tradition to give students inexpensive canvas book bags on the first day of class, and to hand out fabric markers and other supplies the students could use to decorate them. This year, however, I was teaching high school students, and I hesitated. These sophisticated, almost-adult students would undoubtedly see drawing on book bags as hopelessly infantile. So on the first day of class, I passed out the book bags but held onto the markers. "Well," I said, "if you want, you can decorate your book bags—but if that sounds childish to you, fine. I understand." The students practically ripped the markers out of my hands. They set to work intently, covering their book bags with Hebrew words and Jewish symbols, creating elaborate designs; half an hour later, when I suggested that it was time to move on, they passed back the markers reluctantly; several asked if they could borrow some markers for a week and finish their book bags at home.

For some students, art provides ways of expressing ideas, emotions, and enthusiasms they find it difficult to articulate. It's a mistake to think only younger students should do art projects. Older students benefit, too. After all, how many adults find deep satisfaction in drawing, doing needlework, creating scrapbooks, or decorating rooms? It's also a mistake to think we can't plan successful art projects unless we're talented artists ourselves. I can't draw at all—if I need an outline of the Ten Commandments, I have to find something to trace. Even so, I often include art projects in my classes, and I'm convinced students enjoy and

learn from them. They may not learn to be better artists, but that's not the point. We use art to reinforce lessons about Judaism, to give students chances to express their ideas about what they've studied, and to provide them with experiences that will make them more enthusiastic about Judaism. We don't have to be artists to achieve these goals.

Books and websites offer plenty of ideas for projects. Often, the simplest ideas are best. After discussing a prayer, Torah story, or mitzvah, we can just let students draw a picture about what they've learned. An effective art project need not be any more elaborate than that. We can add excitement by adding new materials—paper with unusual texture, paint mixed with glitter, fancy markers.

We should think twice about getting too fancy. Some art projects are essentially teacher-created kits that present students with precut materials and detailed instructions for assembling them. Little room is left, either for mistakes or for the students' own ideas. Students may end up with beautiful objects, but I wonder how much satisfaction they find in creating them.

I've had most luck when I give students general directions and a variety of materials, then just set them loose. Over the years, I've accumulated bags of art supplies by wandering through craft stores and searching through closets, looking for anything that seems attractive or promising or odd. Students love it when I dump out a bunch of stuff on my desk and say, "Make a Sukkot centerpiece/collage about *tikun olam*/Hanukkah present for your parents/Passover mobile." Students happily make their selections from the felt scraps, sequins, ribbon remnants, colored pipe cleaners, bits of tissue paper, pictures cut from magazines or calendars, and uncooked pasta shells; and they concoct sometimes lovely, sometimes bizarre, often provocative creations surpassing anything I'd imagined. It isn't hard to put together art projects if we keep the emphasis on making them enjoyable opportunities for students to express thoughts they've had while we've studied Judaism together.

Sometimes, art projects also enrich students' practice of Judaism at home. Every Passover, my family takes out the matzah cover my older daughter embroidered in her third-grade class and the *afikoman* holder my younger daughter made in kindergarten. My younger daughter is in high school now and has become a skilled artist; every year, she groans when she sees her crude crayon drawings. But I think she'd be disappointed if any other *afikoman* holder ever appeared on our seder table.

It's the same with many other daughters and sons. Jews have a tradition of creating covers for objects associated with religious practice, from *tallitot* to *mezuzot*. When our students make such covers, they may create treasures that will become part of family celebrations for years. Sometimes, a student's art project can be the last gentle nudge a family needs to start observing Judaism more fully at home. A student who learns Hamotzi and makes a ḥallah cover will probably want to use it and to recite the blessing at Shabbat dinner, and many families will gladly oblige. If we also send home a recipe for ḥallah and a handout providing the words to the blessing and some background information, we increase the chances that the art project will have a lasting impact.

One easy, effective project is making folders for Ḥanukkah blessings, the four questions, and other home rituals. Students enjoy decorating such folders and showing off the Hebrew they've learned; again, a student's art project can add to a whole family's religious observance and fulfill the mitzvah of *hiddur mitzvah*—beautifying the commandment. Not long ago, a former student's mother remarked that her family still uses the Shabbat blessings folder her daughter made in class six years ago. I'm glad we took time to do the project.

✕ Music: A Way to Rejoice, A Way to Learn

Perhaps even more than art, music is an important part of our curriculum. Over the centuries, Jews have often expressed ideas and emotions in music. Religious schools are natural places for students to learn about this beautiful part of their heritage. Traditional melodies form a part of our worship; Israeli songs embody our history and express our commitments; contemporary Jewish music addresses the issues we face today and gives voice to our passions. It would be hard to imagine Jewish education without music.

Most larger congregations have cantors or music teachers who lead assemblies and visit individual classes. Such experts provide valuable help; even so, classroom teachers may look for additional ways to use music to underscore lessons. In smaller congregations, classroom teachers may teach music on their own. Clearly, teachers who have strong singing voices or play instruments have an advantage. One teacher I know, an amateur composer as well as a fine guitarist, leads his students in singing every week and helps them write clever songs about *Tanach* stories and holidays.

Those of us who can't carry a tune, much less tune an instrument, can't do that, but we can still make music part of our classes. If our school lacks a music teacher, we can invite talented congregation members to visit our classes, ask these congregants to make tapes of songs, or use commercially produced Jewish tapes and CDs. If our students play instruments, we can invite them to perform. I have fond memories of the time one boy said his middle school band had learned *"Hatikvah"*; could he play it for us? The only problem was that James is a percussionist. It took him ten minutes to set up his drums and cymbals, and his performance consisted of long pauses punctuated by crisp taps and clashes. It was not, perhaps, the most thrilling music lesson in the history of Jewish education. But James enjoyed the spotlight, his classmates applauded enthusiastically, and our discussion of the song was more memorable because it was preceded by a live performance of sorts.

Discussion is a crucial part of every music lesson, particularly when we teach Hebrew songs. Once, a familiar word in a vocabulary lesson made my students burst into a spontaneous rendition of "*David Melech Yisrael.*" They'd mastered the melody, they could pronounce the words, and of course they knew the gestures—but when I asked what the song is about, they had no idea. It's hard to believe no teacher had ever told those students what that song means, but perhaps the meaning hadn't been emphasized enough. As a result, singing "*David Melech Yisrael*" had become, for these students, a superficially pleasant but essentially empty business of parroting meaningless syllables.

We need to teach such songs in ways that deepen our students' understanding of Hebrew and of the ideas and feelings expressed. Among other things, we should usually resist the temptation to use transliterations, instead taking time to help students read lyrics in Hebrew and learn exactly what they mean. For example, suppose we're teaching Debbie Friedman's "*L'chi Lach.*" We can just say the song is about Abraham leaving his native land, then concentrate on helping students learn the melody and pronounce transliterations. Or we can linger over the Hebrew—explaining that *Lech L'cha* is the name of a Torah portion, talking briefly about masculine and feminine forms, pointing out the similarities between words in the song and familiar words such as *simḥah* and *ḥai,* and linking the song to other attempts to honor both matriarchs and patriarchs. In such a context, the song has far more educational value, and students are far more likely to remember what the words mean. A music lesson has also become a Hebrew lesson, a Torah lesson, and a lesson about current Jewish issues—a valuable investment of religious school time, by almost anyone's standard.

✕ Drama: Challenges and Rewards

Like art and music, drama helps students explore ideas and makes lessons memorable. It's also fun. Charades is a quick, lively way to review vocabulary words or *Tanach* stories; role plays help students see how mitzvot can be put into practice; impromptu skits bring a saying from *Pirkei Avot* to life. Informal classroom dramatics take little effort, and almost all students love them.

Almost all students also love performing for an audience. Sometimes, putting on a play involves the full school: A teacher with a background in theater takes charge, students from various classes audition for roles, and other students help with costumes and props. In other schools, plays are left up to individual classes. Preschoolers act out a story while the teacher reads a narration; students write a skit using the conversational Hebrew vocabulary they've learned; a class performs a one-act play for an assembly.

Unlike informal classroom dramatics, plays take lots of work, and the teacher usually ends up doing most of it. Sometimes, we find good plays in anthologies; often, students want to write plays of their own. That generally means students brainstorm ideas and contribute some lines, and the teacher puts the script together. The teacher will also probably be the director and take primary responsibility for props, costumes, and other details; if students do these tasks, plays absorb too much class time. I love putting on plays with my students, but only because I enjoy writing and don't mind sewing costumes and making props while watching television. A teacher who doesn't find such chores fun probably shouldn't put on a play, any more than I should organize a concert.

As directors, teachers have to be sensitive. The focus should be on giving students an enjoyable educational experience, not on putting on a flawless production. When it comes to casting, for example, I recommend cowardice. We can let students choose parts, drawing lots if two or more want the same one. We won't always get the best actors in lead roles, and our plays will be bumpier as a result, but that's probably better than making students feel hurt or resentful because they weren't chosen for the parts they wanted.

For most productions, I also recommend letting students use scripts during performances. We can encourage them to memorize their parts, but we probably can't devote much class time to rehearsing, count on students to practice on their own, or assume parents can transport students to rehearsals outside class time. If students are basically familiar with their parts and don't keep their eyes constantly riveted on their scripts, that's good enough. On the day of the performance, we should be prepared to cope cheerfully with disasters ranging from costumes left at home to stars suddenly coming down with colds. Usually, we can find some way to salvage the production.

Given all the headaches, is putting on a play worth the trouble? I think so, especially if you collaborate with a colleague. Plays provide opportunities for students to work together on a project and have fun in religious school; they give families a chance to enjoy seeing their children on stage; and they make Jewish stories and ideas vivid not only for the actors but also for everyone in the audience. Teachers can enjoy putting on plays, too, as long as we're not perfectionists about it and don't let ourselves get too frustrated by the things that always go wrong. A teacher who has the exacting temperament and high artistic standards needed to succeed as a director in Hollywood should probably stay away from religious school plays.

✕ Games: Channeling Energy, Reinforcing Lessons

For some reason, reviewing Hebrew vocabulary becomes thrilling if we divide a class into teams, draw a tic-tac-toe grid on the blackboard, and let students who pronounce and translate words correctly chalk in *aleph*s or *bet*s. Even students who usually stare at the floor during Hebrew lessons debate answers with teammates in impassioned whispers. The game takes more time than straightforward flashcard reviews—students inevitably waste valuable minutes arguing about where to place the next *aleph* in order to block the *bet* team's strategy. But their pleasure may compensate for the lost minutes, especially if the game gets the students to focus on vocabulary words; too often, in flashcard reviews, a few students compete to call out answers, while the rest listen passively or not at all.

It's easy to adapt favorites such as Concentration, Twenty Questions, or Jeopardy to fit almost any subject; teachers' manuals offer ideas for additional games. Many students would love to turn every lesson into a game, but we know that isn't possible. Most games work better for reviewing than for learning something new, and most emphasize memory rather than thinking ideas through in depth. Occasional games can enliven class and pique students' interest.

Keeping all students interested should be a main objective in any game. That's one reason team games are generally better than those pitting individual students against one another. In individual competition, the potential for humiliation is high, and the same students tend to win time after time. Games built on the spelling-bee model are especially problematic. Students who get eliminated during the early stages have nothing to do but to watch glumly as other students excel—or to act up now that they no longer have a stake in the competition. With teams, everyone has a chance to win until the game ends, and no one has to take a loss personally. To further protect students' feelings (and save time), we can assign teams ourselves, rather than having captains pick teammates. The simplest approaches are pitting one side of the room against the other, or having students count off.

✗ *When High Spirits Get Out of Hand*

Purim parties wouldn't be much fun if participants didn't have energy and high spirits; neither would religious school. If asked why we teach, most of us would say it's partly because we enjoy sharing our knowledge of and love for Judaism, partly because we enjoy our students' company. At our day jobs, most of us have to be staid and serious, strictly focused on business; coming together with a room full of young people is an invigorating change that allows us to indulge our own taste for playfulness.

But we also need to get work done. Four thousand years of Jewish heritage to share, and usually only a few hours a week to do it—religious school is serious business, and some students just can't settle down to it. We joke with them, we play games—and still, whenever we ask students to focus on Hebrew for five minutes, some chat with neighbors or fiddle with any object within reach. They can drive us nuts.

It helps to start by recognizing that most religious school discipline problems are essentially excesses of high spirits—oversupplies of the very qualities that make teaching enjoyable. If students do have serious problems, we of course have to recognize them as such, and to call on the principal, the rabbi, and any other experts we can consult for help. For the most part, however, we don't have to deal with such painful issues as drugs or violence; instead, we have to deal with doodling and smart remarks. We have few if any miniature Hamans in our classes, few if any wicked, wicked students. But we do have many students who find sitting still pure agony.

It also helps if we don't automatically blame ourselves. If we could make classes more interesting, we think, students would pay attention; if we could be more likable—or intimidating—students would show us more respect. We may have read books that say most discipline problems are caused by teachers' mistakes: If students fail to behave, it's because we've failed as teachers.

Undoubtedly, if lessons get truly boring, students are more likely to get restless; if an entire class is constantly out of control, the teacher's doing something wrong. But no teacher can be expected to be spellbinding for two or three hours straight; students should be able to behave even when they find activities less than fascinating. And, in fact, most students can. Some students behave for virtually any class, any teacher; some act up for virtually any class, any teacher. If fifteen students are working steadily, and one or two or several are acting up, it's unreasonable to place all the blame on the teacher. We can consider the possibility that improving our teaching will improve students' behavior, but we needn't assume we're failures.

The next step toward handling classroom management might be to decide what level of discipline we'll try to maintain. Most of us like a relatively relaxed atmosphere—but only relatively. We enjoy good-natured joking around, but we won't allow students to say genuinely disrespectful things to us, or unkind things to each other. If the joking is so constant that the class isn't getting its work done, that's a problem. When discussions get lively, we may let students speak without raising hands—but we won't let them interrupt each other, or us. If students whisper with neighbors or scribble in textbooks, we feel we should intervene. We may have to experiment to find a good balance between order and informality, one that allows us to teach effectively and helps students learn.

Next, we need to make our expectations clear. Some teachers discuss discipline standards on the first day of class, and sometimes that works. I prefer to avoid such discussions on the first day. That's what students get in public school: In every class, teachers pass out lists of rules and punishments. I like doing other things on the first day—talking about the exciting things we'll study, having some fun together, making the tone of class friendlier and more positive.

If behavior problems arise—and they usually do—we can have students help set rules. That sounds risky, but it can work well if we link it to a discussion of Judaism—a story about the covenant, perhaps, or a lesson about a mitzvah such as *kavod*. To use the second example, we can introduce the mitzvah, ask students why respect is important in various situations, then say it's important in class, too. We can ask students what rules promote *kavod* in class, list ideas on the board, perhaps ask students to write rules on a sign we'll post. I give students strips of paper on which to write rules, then paste the strips to the sign.

Even students who act up tend to be fair and sensible when invited to help devise rules; some even propose rules that reflect their own behavior. "Don't get too hyper," one boy suggested sheepishly during a discussion of classroom *kavod*. He was the most hyper person in class, and he obviously knew it. In proposing that rule, he was echoing something parents and teachers had often told him; he knew it was good advice, though he continued to have a tough time following it. So he wrote his rule on a paper strip, and we pasted it to the sign we hung on the wall. There it was—his own rule, in his own words and handwriting—a constant reminder to him, and something I could point to when necessary. It didn't keep him from getting hyper from time to time—probably, no force on earth can do that, not until he outlasts puberty—but it helped.

It helps most students, I think, if they see rules as guidelines they helped develop to handle behavior they themselves recognize as disruptive, not as arbitrary limits imposed in advance by the teacher. Of course, the teacher should take part in the discussion, making sure all necessary guidelines get on the list and steering students away from anything excessive or merely silly. But if students see the process of deciding on rules as partly democratic, they're more likely to abide by the agreed-upon code and help enforce it. ("Look at the list, Ari. We agreed not to interrupt each other—remember? So let me finish my sentence.")

Even the most complete, most accepted list of rules won't stop students from misbehaving occasionally. It's just too hard to keep control, just too much fun to see if a wadded-up tissue can make it all the way to the wastebasket. Sooner or later, we have to deal with disruptive students.

For three years, my husband and I were resident directors of a college dormitory, guided by a wise associate dean. At staff meetings, we and the other directors pelted him with questions—what to do if we saw an empty beer bottle in a student's wastebasket, what to do if we spotted students sneaking out after hours. Whatever problem we mentioned, his advice was the same: "Confront the situation." That seemed maddeningly vague. "But what should we do?" we'd ask. Again, he had an answer—always the same answer: "Do whatever it takes."

In time, we realized he'd given us invaluable advice—advice that applies to religious school, too. When students misbehave, we should confront it. If we pretend not to notice, or let students know we've noticed but won't act, we lose respect—we're either oblivious or cowardly. And when we confront misbehavior, we should do whatever it takes to stop it—nothing less, nothing more.

Let's say that during Hebrew, Danny takes an enormous rubber band from his book bag and begins silently aiming it at other students, stretching it over his face to produce distorted expressions, curiously wrapping it around his wrist to see if he can cut off his circulation. You hear students snickering, and you see what Danny's doing. How should you confront it?

Your primary goal is to keep Danny's antics from making it impossible for you to teach and the class to learn. So you start by doing as little as possible. Sometimes, an exasperated look is enough. You catch Danny's eye and frown briefly; meanwhile, you keep teaching. With luck, Danny will put the rubber band away. Maybe other students noticed what you did, maybe they didn't—it hardly matters. You've eliminated the distraction, moved class ahead, and maintained your authority with the student who challenged it.

If Danny stubbornly keeps toying with the rubber band, you can take things to the next level by walking away from your desk, standing next to him, perhaps putting a hand on his shoulder. You still haven't said a word to him; the lesson is still uninterrupted. If Danny puts the rubber band away now, fine.

If not, you probably need to speak to him. I've found it effective to be elaborately polite, to speak as if we take the student's cooperation for granted. "Danny," you can say, pleasantly, "that rubber band's distracting me. Could you please put it away? Thanks." You don't have to wait for Danny to put the rubber band away before thanking him, and you don't have to prove that rubber bands are bad things, much less that Danny's a bad boy. If you comment on the way Danny's behavior is affecting you, not on the behavior itself or Danny himself, you leave him no room for argument: Once you say the rubber band's distracting you, Danny can't very well say it isn't. And the only thing you really have to accomplish is to get rid of the rubber band. A direct, friendly request generally does it.

Admittedly, if Danny has serious concentration problems or is hell-bent on testing your limits, he may balance a pencil on his nose five minutes later and tape his hand to his desk five minutes after that. Once again, you have to confront the situation and do whatever it takes. Sometimes, a joking reprimand can charm a student into cooperating—as long as the student doesn't see the joke as an invitation to further clowning around. You could also break the mood by putting the lesson aside for the moment and announcing that it's time to visit the library. Or you could set the class to work on a written exercise, take Danny into the hallway for the moment, and talk to him seriously about the way his behavior is disrupting the class. Another choice would be to respond to his antics with something other students will recognize as a punishment—asking him to move his seat, taking away whatever object he's currently disfiguring himself with, telling him to sit in the sanctuary and calm down for five minutes. If the problem continues, you could send Danny to see the principal, or call his parents after class.

Most principals are glad to have serious talks with misbehaving students, and those talks sometimes help. If they don't, religious school principals seldom have many other measures at their disposal. It's hard to give a student detention if it means keeping an entire carpool waiting, and suspending a student may be enough to make a family leave a congregation.

Talking to parents requires tact. We can preface criticisms with positive remarks about how bright the child is and the progress he or she is making; we can say, honestly, that we like the child and want to help him or her enjoy and profit from religious school. When we describe the problem, we can choose our words judiciously. "Exuberant" is preferable to "wild"; "high-spirited" works better than "out of control." We should never exaggerate problems to win sympathy or make a point; if our words and tone are so gentle that parents suspect we're understating the case, they're likelier to be receptive.

It helps that our calls seldom take parents completely by surprise. Usually, students who have behavior problems in religious school have problems in public school, too; chances are, our calls aren't the first ones parents have received. Clearly, it's also important to listen to what parents have to say. Often, they'll have important information to give us. Once, for example, a mother told me that her son had a serious attention disorder and took Ritalin during the week to keep his behavior in public school under control; on weekends, however, she liked to give him a break from medication. No wonder his pent-up energy made him ricochet off the walls of my classroom on Sunday mornings. Having this information helped me understand the student's behavior and respond to him appropriately. We can also look for ways to involve parents in making plans to help students change their behavior. And when a student's behavior does improve, we should be sure to call parents again, to let them know about the improvement and to thank them for their help.

As helpful as principals and parents can sometimes be, I prefer to keep discipline problems within the classroom whenever possible. Involving outside authorities may make students see us as opponents bent on getting them in trouble, and that makes discipline harder in the long run. If there's a secret to keeping order in class, it may be that we have to genuinely like our students—even the ones who act up—and they have to know it. If students know we like them and want them to succeed, they're likelier to want to cooperate. Within that context, most problems can be handled in a friendly way, as situations students and teacher are working out together. When students make progress in getting their behavior under control, we can let them know that we've noticed the change and appreciate their efforts; students need to know that acting up isn't the only way to get our attention. We'll never get all students to behave perfectly all the time, but we can usually find ways to work together with mutual respect and reasonable efficiency.

⊁ *Esther: A Problem Child Turns Out Well*

I wonder what Esther's religious school teachers thought of her. Nothing in the *Megillah* suggests she would have been a model student. As a young woman, she was apparently content to spend a full year in the palace, occupied with nothing more significant than anointing herself with myrrh, perfumes, and ointments. She then married a gentile and concealed her Judaism—she can't have been lighting Shabbat candles. When Mordecai asked her to save her people, Esther's first impulse was to turn him down and save herself. Probably, in her religious school days, she was the sort who fussed with lipstick during lectures on Jewish ethics. She may have excelled at drama—she could play a part well when she deceived Haman—but chances are she yawned through Hebrew. "Not studious," her teachers may have jotted in their notes. "No indication of strong commitment to Judaism or the Jewish community. Undisciplined. Ditzy."

But when it truly counted, Esther came through. She put aside her luxurious ways and fasted; she proved clever enough to trick Haman; she risked her life by speaking to the king; she rescued the Jews of Persia. Maybe her old religious school teachers were surprised when she turned out so well. Then again, maybe not. "Well," they may have said, "she frankly never seemed all that promising, but I never thought she was a bad kid. Undisciplined, yes. Scatterbrained, even—but not bad. And didn't she do a fine job as Jael in the fifth-grade play? Who knows? Maybe that inspired her."

When we look out into the rows of students in our classrooms, we can't know just whom we're seeing: Esthers-in-embryo, perhaps, or Davids-in-development, or future Marc Chagalls, future Debbie Friedmans, future Steven Spielbergs—along with, undoubtedly, many students who will never become famous but will nevertheless contribute to the Jewish community, and come through when it counts. By making our curriculum comprehensive, we offer all of them a variety of ways to excel, a variety of ways to explore and express their growing understanding of and commitment to Judaism. By balancing discipline with patience and good humor, we help make religious school a strong bond connecting all of them to the Jewish people.

✹ SUGGESTED RESOURCES ❧

I'm grateful to Dr. Sherry Feinstein for recommending some of these books, which present general educational theories and techniques in non-technical language and can readily be adapted to meet the needs of the Jewish classroom.

Thomas Armstrong, *Multiple Intelligences in the Classroom*, 2nd edition (Alexandria, Va.: Association for Supervision and Curriculum Development, 1994).

> The author's discussion of various kinds of intelligences—for example, linguistic, logical-mathematical, bodily-kinesthetic, musical, and interpersonal—can help us understand the many different ways in which students learn. Chapters explain how to apply this understanding as we develop curriculum, plan lessons, and handle discipline problems. (The author's website—**www.thomasarmstrong.com**—offers a fascinating, unconventional discussion of attention deficit disorder.)

Shirley Barish, *The Big Book of Great Teaching Ideas for Jewish Schools, Youth Groups, Camps, and Retreats* (New York: URJ Press, 1996).

> This book could be included in the suggested reading list for almost any chapter, for it covers a wide range of topics. I've found it most helpful, however, as a wonderful source of ideas for games, art projects, and ways to use music and drama in the classroom. The activities described in this book can make the study of just about any subject livelier, more active, and more fun for both students and teachers. The suggestions are grouped by age level (kindergarten and primary grades, intermediate grades, junior and senior high school).

C. M. Charles, *Building Classroom Discipline* (Boston: Allyn & Bacon, 2002).

> *Building Classroom Discipline* discusses seventeen models of classroom discipline, identifying their strengths and shortcomings, and shows teachers how these models can be applied in the classroom. Drawing upon these discussions, the author encourages teachers to develop their own approaches to discipline. Jewish teachers will find this book a valuable guide as they look for ways to adapt general theories of classroom management to the situations in their own particular schools and the needs of their own particular students.

5. Passover

FOUR LESSONS FROM A CLASSIC TEXTBOOK

We shall remember. We shall not forget.

Praised is the one who remembers the glory!

Praised is the one who lingers over the telling!

—Rabbi Chaim Stern,
Gates of Freedom: A Passover Haggadah

More than any other event, the outgoing from Egypt defines Judaism. It is the most unequivocal demonstration of God's power, the most dramatic fulfillment of the Covenant; it marks the beginning of our gradual formation into a true people; it leads to the Revelation at Sinai; it culminates in reclaiming our promised home in Israel. If there is one story that we must learn, that we must not fail to pass on to our children, it is this one. How appropriate it is, then, that Jews labored for centuries to create a textbook worthy of teaching this supremely important lesson.

In structure, purpose, and substance, the Haggadah is in many ways our greatest textbook, laying out the lesson plan for a class so important that every Jew must repeat it yearly—the seder. The Haggadah represents the work of generations of our most skilled teachers, drawing on the *Tanach,* the Talmud, the siddur, and other sacred texts that have taught us through the millennia. It embodies the practical knowledge about learning developed during the long history of a people that has always depended on education, not power, to survive. Teachers can find countless insights about teaching in the Haggadah—about the benefits of embracing differing opinions, about using the senses to make ideas concrete, even about the value of taking a break from a long lesson to serve a snack (or, sometimes, a meal). Since it's impossible to explore all these lessons in one chapter, perhaps it's best to follow the Haggadah's example of cutting endless possibilities down to four—four questions, four children, four Passover commandments. Perhaps it's best to focus on four of the lessons the Haggadah teaches us: about the role questions play in learning, the centrality of Jewish history, the importance of the home, and the value of repetition.

✳ *Lesson One: Learning Starts with Questions*

Tradition says the Passover story must be told in response to questions: Unless the youngest present asks the four questions, the seder cannot proceed. Many commentators have observed that, logically, the four questions should come near the end of the seder, to express the curiosity children would feel after seeing only bitter herbs and unleavened bread served, and herbs dipped twice. Before these odd things happen, children would have no reason to wonder why this night is unlike all others. Possibly in early *Haggadot,* the four questions did come later, but were moved up to get children interested—and, perhaps, to underscore the link between questions and education. As our own parents and teachers said to us many times, "If you don't ask, how can you learn?"

But asking questions isn't always easy. As another part of the Haggadah teaches, not all children can ask questions that will lead to the answers they need. We don't have to classify students as wise, wicked, simple, or lacking the wits to ask to appreciate the insights embedded in the story of the four children. Sometimes, students ask perceptive, well-informed questions that lift a discussion to a higher level. Sometimes, they ask mocking questions that reflect a desire to prove how above-it-all they are, not a desire to learn. Sometimes, they ask questions so confused that it's clear the entire class slipped past them in a blur; sometimes, they gaze at us blankly, unable to articulate any questions at all.

The Haggadah teaches that we must respond appropriately to all sorts of questions, all sorts of students. We are told not to shrug off students who ask probing questions, but rather to provide the full answers their questions deserve: "You shall explain all the laws of the Passover, to the last detail about the *afikoman.*" Students who use questions to advertise their attitudes may be answered in ways that let them know we see through their act—but still give them the information they're too cool to admit they want. ("So, what are pogroms?" the student asked, smirking. "Some kind of fruit?" "I think you know pogroms aren't fruits," the teacher said, allowing herself an exasperated sigh. "I think you know they're a painful part of our history. Why don't you turn to page 127 and summarize the second paragraph in your own words? Then we'll all know what pogroms are.") Students whose questions reflect their confusion should receive clear, simple answers that let them know they're valued members of the group: "With a strong hand the Eternal brought *us* out of Egypt." When students say nothing, we must, as the Haggadah says, take the lead, nudging them toward the questions they don't know how to ask.

The Haggadah doesn't rely on children to come up with the four questions on their own. Rather, it spells the questions out, and generations of children have found merely reading the questions both a challenge and a source of pride. Sometimes we too may provide students with questions, by picking textbooks that include discussion questions or devising our own questions to accompany assignments.

Sometimes we may use the Haggadah's techniques to prod students to ask questions. Just as we load the seder plate with unusual objects likely to pique a child's curiosity, we can use intriguing physical objects in class. We, or a guest, can silently demonstrate the process of laying tefillin and wait for the questions to start; we can give students pencils and pads, take them to the sanctuary, and invite them to explore and to jot down questions about anything that strikes them as beautiful or odd. Showing clips from movies about Jewish families and Jewish life can also stimulate questions about customs and beliefs.

Of course, we're bound to ask questions ourselves. Asking questions is probably the most common technique for testing students' understanding, for motivating them to examine ideas more thoroughly, for encouraging them to articulate ideas or express opinions, and for helping them challenge us or each other or themselves. We all know to avoid questions that can be answered with a simple "yes" or "no," that students grow frustrated if they realize a teacher is fishing for one predetermined answer, and that the best questions encourage students to think for themselves. Yet coming up with the right questions can be as hard for teachers as it is for students. I like to write out at least some questions in advance, so I can try to get the wording right and to ask questions that help students focus on developing their own ideas.

Responding to students' answers can be tricky, too. We generally know more than our students do, and it's tempting to show our knowledge off by proving we can answer questions more fully than they can. Usually, it's a temptation we're wise to resist. When a student gives us a good-enough answer, we can accept it, praise it, perhaps challenge the student to explore it further. Suppose we ask a class who Abraham was, and a student answers that he was the first Jew. Should we respond by immediately pointing out that the word "Jew" is technically incorrect in this context, that it didn't come into usage until long after Abraham died, and that it would be more accurate to describe Abraham as the first Hebrew? What do we gain through such a response? We've introduced a distinction that will probably strike most of the class as a quibble; meanwhile, we've embarrassed the student who answered the question and given everyone else a good reason to think twice before taking the risk of speaking up. After all, Abraham was the founder of our religion, the first partner in our Covenant with God. Why not respond to the student's answer by saying, "Good! We *do* think of Abraham as the first Jew. Why? Why do we say Abraham was the first Jew—rather than Noah, for example, or Moses?" This answer should leave the student feeling affirmed and proud, and it may lead the group into a valuable discussion of what it means to be a Jew. Later, if we like, we can point out the difference between "Jew" and "Hebrew"—but we can mention it as a new bit of information, not as a correction to the student's answer. The student's answer was fine; we can safely let it stand.

What should we do when answers are flat-out wrong? "As the people of Israel traveled to Sinai," the teacher says, "they sometimes disagreed with each other, and they always brought their disagreements to Moses. The Torah says they crowded around him from morning until evening, insisting he answer every question that came up. Moses' father-in-law, Jethro, saw it was tiring Moses out. So Jethro made a suggestion. What was it?" Tentatively, a student raises her hand. "That's when the Talmud got started, right? Jethro saw the Jews needed a better way of settling arguments, so he told Moses to write the Talmud."

It's easy to shoot this answer down. "No. Moses did *not* write the Talmud, and Jethro never suggested he do any such thing. The Talmud is a commentary on the Torah. This incident happened on the way to Sinai—remember? We didn't even have the Torah yet, so how could Jethro tell Moses to write a commentary about it? You're off by more than a thousand years."

That response is easy. But it's not too hard to give a response that sets matters straight without making the student feel like a fool. "Interesting answer, Susannah. You're right—the Talmud *does* try to settle disagreements and answer questions. Another interesting thing about the Talmud is that many people worked on it together—the Talmud doesn't leave everything up to just one person. Those are two important Jewish traditions—trying to answer questions, and getting opinions from more than one person. The Talmud itself wasn't actually written until after Moses' time, but maybe Jethro's suggestion helped start the tradition that led to the Talmud. That's a fascinating comparison—it never occurred to me before. Thanks, Susannah. You've really got me thinking. Now, what was the specific suggestion that Jethro made, the one that helped start the tradition of getting lots of people involved in answering questions?"

This response lets Susannah know she hasn't zeroed in on the precise answer to this question, but it also recognizes what's good about her answer. In fact, her superficially absurd answer probably *did* originate in some glimmering of similarities between the first judges and the rabbis who created the Talmud. If we can see past the anachronism, we can reassure Susannah about the value of her insight and help the whole class see the story in a broader, richer context.

It's not so difficult, not if we assume that even flat-out wrong answers often contain a grain of something right—some bit of information the student picked up or some potentially interesting idea the student has. Responding to excellent answers takes care, too. We want to praise the answer, but not so extravagantly that the student gets embarrassed or other students get jealous. In almost any class, some students give better answers than others. If we're not careful, praise of these answers can look like favoritism for these students. And we don't want to play into the hands of the occasional students who answer questions to demonstrate their superiority and make others feel inadequate.

We can compensate for such problems by not calling on the same students every time, even if the same hands always shoot up first. We can look past those hands, make questions more detailed, give other students more time to think and other hands more courage to venture up. We can also find ways to compliment all students, not just those who answer most accurately. We shouldn't withhold praise when Ruth answers yet another question well, but we can also notice and praise when Brian blends colors expertly in his picture about Noah, or when Tracy helps a younger student follow the Hebrew during children's services.

When we do praise excellent answers, we can make our praise so specific that it helps all students learn how to excel: "That's right, Alex. You must have read the assignment carefully to remember those details." "Great, Leah. I love the comparison with Hillel. That shows you paid close attention last week, and kept thinking about the ideas we discussed." Students get a special glow when we say they've asked a question that never occurred to us or seen a connection we never sensed: "Wow! You're right—I never noticed that before." We lose nothing by making such admissions. Students won't think we're ignorant, only that we're unusually perceptive for recognizing their brilliance.

If we're concerned about over-praising students who stand out, we can keep public praise moderate and magnify it through after-class comments, phone calls, or e-mail messages: "I've been thinking about your comment on the Balfour Declaration—the more I think about it, the more I like it. It shows shrewd insight into the political situation at the time." Praise relayed by parents may please students even more than praise given directly. If we really want to reward and motivate students, we can call parents and say, "Josh asked a fascinating question—about why we say 'Abraham, Isaac, and Jacob,' not 'Abraham, Isaac, and Israel.' He's always coming up with original, perceptive questions that make us all think harder and learn more." We can be sure that the compliment will make its way to Josh and that he'll come to the next class more determined than ever to ask original, perceptive questions. Parents love it when we praise their children for giving excellent answers; I think they love it even more when we praise their children for asking excellent questions. Maybe that's because parents realize, as we do, that asking questions is a crucial first step in the long journey toward learning about Judaism.

✳ *Lesson Two: The Importance of Jewish History*

History isn't the most glamorous part of the Jewish curriculum or the easiest to sell to students—or, sometimes, to teachers. "I don't waste time trying to get students excited about stuff that happened centuries ago," a teacher once said at a staff meeting. "They couldn't care less, and no wonder. They've got so many decisions bearing down on them right now, today—about sex, drugs, even cheating on tests. I'd rather invest time in talking about *those* things. That's what they *need* to learn." It's a compelling argument. We have to teach students the Hebrew they need to do well at bar or bat mitzvah services; we want them to get involved in community service; we want to give them opportunities to enjoy music, art, and drama. It's tempting to make history just an occasional footnote, to devote most of our time to subjects that seem far more pleasant, far more pressing.

And yet the Haggadah, echoing the Torah, insists we must teach history: "You shall tell your child on that day: 'This is done because of that which the Eternal did for me when I came forth out of Egypt.'" Four times in Exodus and Deuteronomy, we are reminded of the obligation to teach our children about the Exodus from Egypt (in Exodus 12:26, 13:8, and 13:14, and in Deuteronomy 6:20). The Haggadah takes this obligation to heart, dwelling lovingly on the story, debating the interpretation of details, emphasizing central themes repeatedly. Shaped by the conviction that no Jew can afford to stay ignorant about this crucial event, the Haggadah uses every possible means to drive its lesson home.

Nor can we afford to stay ignorant about the rest of our story. As we all know, Judaism means more than learning a set of theological opinions—it also means participating in the life of a people. We cannot truly be part of that life unless we know our people's history. Over time, students who learn about Jewish history develop a deeper understanding of their beliefs, a firmer pride in their heritage, and a stronger loyalty to their people.

And our students have questions that can be answered only through studying Jewish history. "Why do people hate us?" a high school student asked, her voice growing almost childish with hurt. "I mean, we're nice—why are they mean to us? Why did the Holocaust happen?" Students need to learn our history so they can move past merely feeling hurt, so they can shake off the horrible suspicion that there might in fact be something wrong with Jews.

It's tempting to think we can safely leave the teaching of history to the public schools. After all, students take social studies courses every year; won't those courses teach them all the history they need? But few public schools have much time to devote to Jewish history, and many public school teachers don't have the necessary background. In 1992, I taught several workshops on multicultural education to public school teachers. Since it was the 500th anniversary of Columbus's voyage, many articles had come out advising teachers about how to discuss this event with students. Thinking this would be a good topic to cover in the workshops, I read quite a few of these articles. All stressed the importance of looking at Columbus's arrival not only from a European perspective but also from the perspective of indigenous peoples. All warned that talk of Columbus's courage and Isabella's generosity should be balanced by facts about Columbus's ruthlessness and Isabella's greed. Many articles argued that African perspectives should be presented as well, that connections should be drawn with the development of the slave trade. Not a single article pointed out that in 1492 the Jews were expelled from Spain; not one said that Jewish views of Isabella deserved to be mentioned. When I asked the teachers in my workshops about the expulsion from Spain, they stared back incredulously. Not one had heard of the expulsion. Some seemed amused by the idea that Jews had ever lived in Spain at all.

We also can't assume that public schools will handle the job of teaching our students about Jewish accomplishments. A few years ago, my daughter Rachel indignantly showed me a page from her middle school social studies textbook. The introductory page in a chapter about immigration, it featured a dramatic photograph of the Statue of Liberty, with the closing lines from "The New Colossus" superimposed. Emma Lazarus was cited as the author, but not a word about her ancestry was included. "Why doesn't it say Emma Lazarus was Jewish?" Rachel demanded. "Isn't that an important thing to know?" Yes, it's important, especially since the chapter stressed the idea that America has been a refuge for people persecuted and denied opportunities in their native lands. How completely natural, how utterly beautiful and poignant, it would be to point out that the woman who wrote the poem on the base of the Statue of Liberty was the descendant of Jews driven from their home because of their religion. But the book remained silent about Emma Lazarus's Judaism. If we want our students to know Emma Lazarus was Jewish, we'd better tell them ourselves.

True, they may not seem to care. They may not seem interested in Jewish history, or in American history, or in history of any sort. It's tempting to think today's students are uniquely indifferent to history, caught up as they are in their own times and lives. But history has probably always been a hard sell for young people. We might think of Huckleberry Finn's response when Widow Douglas teaches him about Moses: Huck is eager to learn until he realizes Moses has been dead "a considerable long time; so then I didn't care no more about him; because I don't take no stock in dead people."

Huck's attitude has an ancient precedent. As various commentators have said, in its original context the wicked child's question wasn't presented as wicked, just as the natural response of a person who wasn't alive during the Exodus. Moses tells the people how to teach children born in the Promised Land about Passover: "When, in time to come, your children ask you, 'What mean the exhortations, laws, and rules which Adonai our God has enjoined upon you?' you shall say to your children, We were slaves in Egypt, and Adonai freed us from Egypt with a mighty hand'" (Deuteronomy 6:20). Children who have never been slaves and have never been delivered will naturally think of slavery and deliverance as things that happened to other people, not as things relevant to their own lives.

It's an almost inevitable attitude for young people to take. We don't have to condemn it, but we do have to deal with it. The Haggadah tells us how: "In every generation, we are obliged to regard ourselves as though we ourselves had actually gone out of Egypt." As teachers, we search for ways to make our students see and feel that Jewish history is indeed *their* history, that the stories we tell them are part of their own lives. We can borrow techniques from the Haggadah, such as using first-person plural pronouns: "*We* were slaves," "Adonai freed *us*." We can do this, subtly but consistently, when we talk about any event in Jewish history: "After we were expelled from Spain, many of us found new homes in South America." Our students may not consciously notice the pronouns, but they'll get the point: These stories are their stories, our stories, stories that touch the lives of all Jews at all times.

To further underscore the relevance of Jewish history, we teach ideas as well as facts. Facts—names and dates—are undeniably important. Students need to learn about our great leaders and thinkers, to hear about events that shaped our past, and to develop a sense of what happened when. Even in years when I'm not officially teaching history, I usually end up taping a timeline to the wall of my classroom so that when references to people and events come up, students can see how they fit into the continuing story of the Jewish people.

As the Haggadah shows us, however, facts aren't enough. It begins the story of the Exodus twice. The first version reports the facts: "We were slaves of Pharaoh in Egypt, and the Eternal our God brought us out." The second telling stresses the story's spiritual significance: "Long, long ago our ancestors were worshippers of idols," it starts, putting the Exodus into the larger context of the transition from idolatry to monotheism, of the Covenant between God and Israel. The Haggadah is proof that the facts of Jewish history become truly compelling only when they're connected to Jewish ideas and beliefs.

We can draw similar connections in our classes. For example, we can use *Tanach* stories to illustrate the idea that Jewish history has always been shaped by the beliefs that God is One and that God's *mitzvot* teach us how to live, by a sense of peoplehood, by the idea of covenant, and by devotion to the Land of Israel. We can then build on these concepts as we introduce students to stories and figures from later stages in Jewish history. Inevitably, suffering becomes part of the story as students learn about the destruction of the Temples, exile from the Promised Land, persecution, and discrimination. We can balance the undeniable sadness by stressing accomplishments as well as adversities, using every story to underscore the idea that Jews never accepted the role of mere victims. As students build an overview of Jewish history, we can emphasize the central idea that through the centuries Jews have contributed to and been influenced by many places and peoples, accommodating themselves to new situations without surrendering their essential Jewish identity. By organizing the study of Jewish history around such ideas, we help students see our people's story as more than a series of confusing and often distressing incidents. By relating every lesson to themes such as Covenant, resilience, and identity, we give our students a solid basis for seeing all of Jewish history as directly relevant to their own lives. In these ways, our classes can contribute to our students' sense of the richness and complexity of Jewish history, to their pride in belonging to a people that has endured for so long and accomplished so much, and to their determination to be among those who will decide the direction Jewish history takes in the future.

✳ *Lesson Three: Respecting the Home As the Center of Jewish Education*

These days, many synagogues have congregational seders, and many religious schools hold model seders. Such seders help meet the needs of many seniors and singles, of congregations who enjoy celebrating the second (or even third) night of Passover together, and of students who will appreciate the first night more if they're prepared. We know such seders, however valuable, are merely substitutes for or supplements to the real thing. The Haggadah makes it clear that the ideal setting for the year's single most important educational experience is neither the synagogue nor the school. It is the home.

Judaism is a home-based religion, even more than a synagogue-based one. Home observance is a part—often the most important one—of almost every holiday. Ordinary days, too, offer constant opportunities to practice Judaism in the home—reciting blessings at meals, praying together at bedtime, discussing religious and ethical questions, performing a variety of *mitzvot*, reading Jewish stories together. Actively Jewish homes teach Judaism more effectively, constantly, and beautifully than even the finest school.

But it's no revelation to say that many students don't live in actively Jewish homes. As teachers, we may feel our efforts are undermined by the lack of observance in students' homes and by families' apparent indifference to Jewish education. How are Shabbat blessings to seem like anything but abstractions to students if parents never light candles at home? Why should students take our lessons seriously if parents pull them out of class for soccer practice?

We may decide that involving parents in their children's education and motivating them to observe Judaism more fully at home are crucial parts of our work. We may keep parents informed by mailing them letters and syllabi in September, sending students home with notes about what they've done in class, writing articles for the synagogue bulletin, and using report cards, conferences, phone calls, and e-mail messages. We can be scrupulous about keeping in touch when things are going well, not only when students are failing tests or misbehaving. We can invite parents to speak to the class and ask them to help with holiday celebrations. We can have families fill out questionnaires to learn about members' talents and interests, or to find out who's planning a trip to Israel and may come back with photographs to share. We can invite parents and children to create family histories or do *tzedakah* projects together. And any time we get students excited about a Jewish custom, we increase the chance they'll ask parents to give that custom a try. All of these approaches to encouraging family education and involvement can have a positive, significant effect.

But we have to be careful. Our efforts are most likely to be successful if they're tactful and genuinely considerate. An assignment asking students to interview parents about Ḥanukkah memories from childhood may embarrass parents who are converts or gentiles; rewarding students with points if their families say Shabbat blessings may seem intrusive or patronizing. Our emphasis should be on informing families, not reforming them. We provide families with many opportunities and much support—and then we step back and let families make their own decisions. Sincerely respecting the family as the center of Jewish education means recognizing that the religious school does not have the right to tell parents how they should practice Judaism in their own homes. When parents seem unresponsive, we can comfort ourselves with the hope that our efforts have made students more likely to create actively Jewish homes when they head their own families some day.

Can we offer parents encouragement and guidance? Certainly. One year, when our religious school planned a Passover family education event, our central goal was to provide families with information and objects they could use to enrich their home seders. We organized our learning stations around the four questions. At the first station, groups of parents and children learned about the symbolic significance of matzah, then made *afikoman* covers they could use at home. The second station focused on the bitterness of being a slave or a stranger; after talking with a counselor who worked at a center for immigrants and refugees, families decorated appointment calendars that would be added to the welcome kits given to local newcomers to the United States. At the station devoted to the third question, families painted small bowls that could be used for salt water; at the fourth station, they decorated pillow covers that could help them recline in style as they sat around their seder tables. Then we all relaxed and chatted at a farewell-to-*ḥametz* buffet, indulging in the cookies and bagels and doughnuts that would be forbidden to us in a few days. Participation in the event was excellent, and both parents and students seemed excited about what they had learned and the things they had made. All the leftover pillow covers were eagerly claimed by people who said they wanted to decorate some extras when they got home.

Our hope, obviously, was that families would use their new *afikoman* covers, salt-water bowls, and pillow covers at their home seders, and that some of the new insights they had gained would add to their discussions during dinner. Probably, some families used the objects and information in exactly the way we wished; probably, other families put the objects aside as soon as they got home, and didn't have seders at all; possibly, some families who weren't yet confident enough or motivated enough to have seders at home took out those objects a year or two later, when they felt ready. And quite possibly, some families didn't use any of the objects or information from our event because they already had well-established seder customs of their own, customs that might well be, for those particular families, more beautiful and meaningful than anything our religious school staff could devise. In any case, we teachers had done our job. We had given parents and children a chance to enjoy and learn about Judaism together, we had given them information they could use and options to consider, and we had given them an opportunity to create objects that might or might not become part of their family celebrations for years to come. Equally important, we had not tried to pressure anyone into complying with our ideas about what a seder should be. No one had any reason to feel embarrassed or resentful about anything that had happened that morning; it had been a positive experience for everyone—parents, students, and teachers.

Not all family education efforts will leave us with such positive feelings. One year, as principal, I tried what seemed like a perfect way of involving parents in Jewish Book Month. In the temple bulletin and in flyers sent home, I invited parents to visit their children's classes during November to read a Jewish story out loud or report on a Jewish book. There, I thought. During the course of a month, any parent can find ten free minutes—what an easy, painless way to get involved.

But only a few parents participated. Some classes got one visit from a parent willing to read; most got none. My first impulse was to complain about the laziness of parents who want their children to get a Jewish education but won't make even token efforts to help. When I calmed down, I realized I'd been too harsh. To some parents, reading a story out loud might not seem easy and painless. Some might have doubted their ability to read with expression or to pick an appropriate story. Some might have been discouraged by children who thought it would be uncool to have their parents in class. Some parents might have been distracted by problems I knew nothing about, so that the month slipped by before they could pick a story or arrange a time to visit. And some parents might have thought the whole idea was dumb. It's unreasonable to expect all parents to regard all of our ideas as brilliant; we can't assume only laziness could keep them from accepting all of our invitations.

In all our dealings with parents, it's appropriate to be modest as well as tactful. We need to recognize the limits of our own understanding and to respect each family's right to privacy. Even in small congregations, we can't—and shouldn't—know what's happening in all our students' homes at all times; we can't always know parents' reasons for making the choices they do. "Happy families are all alike," Tolstoy writes in *Anna Karenina*. "Every unhappy family is unhappy in its own way." With this statement, Tolstoy does a disservice to happy families. Each happy family is unique, too, and no family is so completely happy that it doesn't face sorrows and challenges. As teachers, we hear about some problems—usually the more spectacular ones such as deaths and divorces. But every day dozens of things go on in our students' families: Relationships are tested, disappointments are endured, situations change, and we don't know a thing about it. We can speculate and generalize, and we can let families know that we're always ready to listen and to help. But if families choose to keep their troubles and their opinions to themselves, we can't really know why this student's homework isn't done this week, or why that family never shows up for Purim carnivals. Even if we're parents ourselves, we can have only a general idea of the challenges other parents face. And we may have only vague, theoretical notions about the challenges faced by parents whose spouses don't share a commitment to Jewish education, by single parents, by same-sex parents, by grandparents raising grandchildren.

May we be sensitive to the needs of all these parents and grandparents; may we resist the temptation to judge any of them. And may we never do anything to weaken their children's respect. Jewish schools meeting on weekends, afternoons, or evenings are often called supplemental schools, in the sense that the work is supplemental to teaching done in public schools. Perhaps all Jewish schools, no matter how often they meet, should think of themselves as supplemental in the sense that we exist to supplement and support work done at home. May we never be so arrogant as to see parents as the source of all problems, ourselves as the source of all solutions.

We can, indeed, hope to be a force for good in our students' lives. My own religious school teachers were a force for good in my life, and I remember them with affection and gratitude. But we're not the ones who influence students most deeply; parents and grandparents do that. We can support their efforts with our special knowledge of certain subjects; we can offer guidance when appropriate. But we cannot take their place, so we must not undermine their authority.

Judaism knows this. It devotes one of the Ten Commandments to reminding children to honor parents; it places the seder in the home because it knows parents can and should be their children's primary teachers. It's our job to do all we can to help parents fulfill this sacred responsibility, using all the skill, tact, modesty, and respect we have.

✳ Lesson Four: "Even Were We All Wise, All Learned in Torah"

"Do we have to study holidays *again*?" students sometimes complain. "We already know all that stuff. Can't we learn something new?"

On one level, we can respond by saying that of course we'll learn something new. Yes, we may cover holidays every year, but we don't cover them in the same way in kindergarten as we do in high school. In one class, we may stress symbols, songs, and games; in another, we may stress holidays' historical origins, or the way they're celebrated in Israel. And the holidays are never the only things we cover. In any class, some new books will be used, some new topics will be introduced, and some new ground will be covered. The myth that religious schools do nothing but review the holidays year after year is popular among students, but we know it isn't true.

On another level, we can answer students by pointing out they do not, in fact, "already know all that stuff." To prove our point, we can ask what "Ḥanukkah" means ("rededication"). Chances are, in any class at any level, few if any students will know—not because no teacher ever told them, but because they've forgotten. And so, year after year, we review the basics. The Haggadah provides us with a precedent by repeating the basics of the Passover story, insisting no one is exempt from the requirement to retell this story every year. Even if we were all wise and learned in Torah, the Haggadah says, even if we were all old and people of understanding, it would still be our duty to take part in this retelling.

This emphasis on repetition should comfort us. Too often, we plan a class carefully, present it skillfully, use creative teaching techniques to get ideas across, and see students' eyes brighten with excitement and new insight—and then we come back next week and see how little has been retained. When we get frustrated, it's good to remember even the Haggadah doesn't count on making its lesson stick the first time. It tells a dramatic story, it uses touch and taste and smell to make the story vivid, it enlivens the experience with anecdotes and songs, it offers mnemonic devices to help us remember—but it knows we'll still forget. So the Haggadah insists that we must, year after year, review the basics.

Yet we don't *just* review the basics. One of the most charming parts of the Haggadah tells of the time some of our greatest rabbis got so caught up in retelling the story of the Exodus that they stayed up all night, and had to be summoned by their students when the time came for morning prayers. The sages didn't spend all those hours going over the basic facts of the story. Instead, they searched the text for new meaning, seeking to make their interpretations fuller and more valuable. We hear bits of their conversation—about the meaning of the phrase "all the days of your life," or the number of plagues inflicted on the Egyptians. Their debates may seem trivial, but they underscore major themes—about the never-ending obligation to retell the Passover story, about the magnitude of God's power and devotion. It's inspiring to see how inventive these rabbis can be when they tease new meanings from a thoroughly familiar text.

The Haggadah isn't the only place where we find an emphasis on returning to the same texts again and again. Simhat Torah celebrates our determination to keep rereading the Torah; Purim centers on the rereading of the *Megillah;* and each year, during the period when we count the Omer, we once again study the seemingly simple sayings in *Pirkei Avot.* The conviction that we have much to learn from continually returning to basic texts is central to Judaism.

That's one reason we keep teaching. We may teach Torah one year, Prophets and Writings the next; we may try new textbooks or new approaches to Hebrew; we may switch from one grade level to another. Still, we do end up covering much of the same material again and again.

Yet it never gets old for us. In searching for better ways to present familiar material to the next group of students, we read new commentaries, explore new websites, exchange new ideas with other teachers. Year after year, as we return once again to the same material, our teaching skills increase—and so does our understanding of our people's basic texts. Teaching religious school is one of the best ways of fulfilling our obligations to the next generation of Jews; it's also one of the best ways to keep growing as Jews ourselves. The Haggadah is one of the many adult education textbooks that guide us as, year after year, we keep teaching, keep learning.

❧❉ SUGGESTED RESOURCES ✦❧

Sheila Rosenblum, ed., *Leadership Skills for Jewish Educators: A Casebook* (West Orange, NJ: Behrman House, 1993).

> Although this book is designed primarily for school administrators, any Jewish educator can find in its pages many useful insights and techniques. The section on relating to parents and students, for example, contains several case studies focusing on the challenges of actively and positively involving parents in their children's education. Discussing these case studies at a staff meeting could be a good opportunity for administrators and teachers to share ideas and perspectives.

Noam Zion and David Dishon, *The Leader's Guide to the Family Participation Haggadah: A Different Night* (Jerusalem: Shalom Hartman Institute, 1997)

> This guide offers the educator information and ideas that can be used in Passover family-education events and other sorts of programs, as well as in lessons related to the holiday. Features include "practical suggestions for managing a participatory seder with children and adults of different ages," short essays containing background information, and examples of creative activities that will help students and their families gain a fuller understanding of holiday themes and traditions.

❧❉ WEBSITE ✦❧

Dinur Center for Research in Jewish History
www.hum.huji.ac.il/dinur

> Teachers looking for ideas about how to teach Jewish history will find much they can use at this site, created by the Dinur Center for Research in Jewish History at the Hebrew University in Jerusalem. There are links to more than 6,000 websites about Jewish history, all visited by Dinur

Center staff members and found to be worthwhile. For example, if you click on "Periods and Topics," you'll find subheadings such as "Second Temple and Talmudic Era" and "American Jewish History"; these in turn will lead you to timelines, bibliographies, and book reviews, as well as hundreds of other links that can enrich your classes. This site also provides links to databases, journals, maps, atlases, discussion groups, archives, museums, and exhibits. Getting students interested in Jewish history will always be a challenge, but we can now take advantage of a world of resources that our own teachers could not have imagined.

✳ 6. Shavuot

CELEBRATING A LIFE OF MITZVOT

Sinai is more than the receiving of the Torah—it is the experiencing of the Divine, an experience shared by all Jews of all time, for each of us was there and heard the Voice of Sinai. While theologians and scholars may debate what actually happened at Sinai, for the religious Jew Sinai is central to both belief and practice—to belief in a God who cares about this world and expects us to strive in our lives to practice what is good and just.

—Michael Strassfeld,
The Jewish Holidays: A Guide and Commentary

Over the years, most of the textbooks I used when I attended religious school have disappeared—worn out, lost, or given away, perhaps in some cases still tucked away in forgotten boxes in my mother's house. About half a dozen textbooks, however, are so precious that I could never part with or lose track of them. The most treasured is William Silverman's *The Still, Small Voice* (New York: Behrman House, 1957), a book that combines a profound introduction to Jewish ethics with the liveliness and charm of a novel. I studied it in class, reread it for enjoyment several times while I was growing up, and have returned to it often as both a mother and a teacher. I'd guess many other Jewish educators working today share my fondness for this textbook; I'd guess many of you still remember the book's opening scene.

Rabbi Mayer is giving his religious school class a history quiz when he notices one of his best students, Jonathan, glancing at a crumpled-up sheet of paper on the floor. The Rabbi asks Jonathan to bring him the paper and sees it's a crib sheet. Embarrassed, Jonathan protests he isn't the only cheater in class—he's just the first to get caught. When most of Jonathan's classmates confess their guilt through silence and downcast looks, Rabbi Mayer tells them all to throw their tests away and says that in a sense he, too, is guilty. "I have tried to teach you the facts of Jewish history, Jewish literature, and Jewish ceremonies," the rabbi says. "But I have failed to impress you with the purpose of Jewish history, literature, and ceremonies." And so he puts his regular curriculum aside, and devotes the rest of the year to teaching his students about Jewish ethics.

It's not hard for us to understand Rabbi Mayer's decision. As Jewish educators, we want to give students the knowledge they'll need to understand their heritage. We want to help them acquire the skills to continue their study of Judaism long after religious school ends, to participate fully in their congregations and communities, and to some day become parents and teachers who in turn can pass on what they've learned to the next generation of Jews. But even if we accomplish all this, we know we haven't truly done our jobs unless we've also helped our students become people with a clear sense of personal ethics, habits firmly grounded in righteous actions, and a strong commitment to social justice. We know we haven't really done our jobs unless we've helped each student become a blessing to the Jewish people and to all the world—until we've helped each student become a *mensch*.

Traditionally, Judaism teaches that one becomes this kind of person by adhering to the *mitzvot*—the Ten Commandments, the other 603 commandments in the Torah, the oral law recorded in the Talmud, and the later rabbinic writings considered authoritative. Our academic year is framed by holidays expressing our gratitude for Torah and *mitzvot*— Simhat Torah in the fall, Shavuot in the spring. The Torah speaks of Shavuot only as an agricultural festival, but over the centuries it has also come to be a time of thanksgiving for the *mitzvot*. During Passover, we begin counting the days and weeks it took the people of Israel to walk from Egypt to Sinai; on the first night of Shavuot, we may stay up all night studying Torah, readying ourselves for the day that sealed the Covenant. We may decorate the synagogue with greenery, not only to celebrate the harvest but also to honor Sinai, which, according to tradition, bloomed green in the desert on the day the Law was given. At services, we read the section of the Torah describing the Revelation at Sinai, perhaps rising when the Ten Commandments are read to relive the experience of those who stood to hear those commandments proclaimed by God. All these customs express Judaism's deep reverence for the *mitzvot* that teach us to lead righteous, holy lives that will be fulfilling for us, beneficial to others, and pleasing to our Creator.

Our students may question the traditional view of the *mitzvot*— indeed, we may question it ourselves. Some branches of Judaism question the whole concept of Revelation; others hold that some truths were revealed at Sinai but question the belief that all of the Torah and the Talmud convey the word of God. Once we raise questions about the divine origin of the *mitzvot,* questions about their authority also inevitably arise. Do we teach our students that all the *mitzvot* Judaism has traditionally revered are binding on all Jews, that they are the one infallible basis for an ethical life? Or do we present the *mitzvot* as partially or completely human creations that are worthy of respect but open to challenge and reinterpretation? If we depart from the traditional view of the *mitzvot,* how do we get students to take them seriously as guides to ethical living?

Others are eager to tell our students that the very idea of living by *mitzvot* is confining and misguided. Christianity, for example, tells them that those who take Jesus into their hearts will lead good lives unfettered by exacting, picayune laws and regulations. We tell our students Torah is a tree of life (Proverbs 3:18); Paul, in 2 Corinthians, dismisses the Revelation at Sinai as "the dispensation of death, carved in letters on stone." Those who follow Jesus, he says, are "ministers of a new covenant, not in a written code but in the Spirit; for the written code kills, but the Spirit gives life" (2 Cor. 3:3, 6–7). In Galatians, Paul declares that "Christ redeemed us from the curse of the law," so that "we might receive the promise of the Spirit through faith" (Gal. 3: 13–14). Our students may hear these quotations from missionaries. They'll definitely encounter the popular, appealing idea that the redeemed have no need of a detailed legal code, that their hearts will show them the difference between right and wrong.

Sooner or later, students also encounter the idea that there's no such thing as right and wrong at all, that no objective standard for distinguishing between ethical and unethical action exists. Few students will read Nietzsche or present sophisticated arguments in favor of moral relativism, but many will absorb the notions that there are no absolute truths, that it's impossible to know what's right and what isn't, that all opinions are equally valid, that being an individual is better than conforming to any code, that personal choice is a sacred right—if, indeed, anything can be called sacred. Therefore, everyone is free to do whatever feels good. This idea can be even more appealing than the idea that the redeemed are free to do whatever feels right. Among other things, it's just so delightfully easy. Every argument can be settled by asserting it's all a matter of opinion; every criticism of one's actions can be defused by asserting it's all a matter of choice.

In times deeply influenced by such ideas, how do we teach our students about Jewish ethics? How do we help our students lead good lives? In part, our answer will depend on the branch of Judaism to which our school or synagogue subscribes and to the view of Revelation we ourselves accept. But I think it can be argued that all Jewish educators, regardless of their religious school affiliation or their own opinions, share an obligation to help their students understand and respect traditional Jewish teachings about *mitzvot*. It's easy these days for many students to dismiss all such teachings as merely silly and inhibiting. Even if we don't accept every facet of traditional Judaism ourselves, we're obliged, I think, to help students see that their heritage is not mindless or contemptible, that there is value and beauty in the *mitzvot* that have shaped countless Jewish lives through the millennia.

One way of helping students appreciate that value and beauty is by emphasizing action as well as ideas. "We will do, and we will listen," the people of Israel said at Sinai (Exodus 24:7). Doing comes first. When we teach *mitzvot*, we will, of course, introduce our students to controversies, engage them in discussions of theoretical issues, and try to answer their questions. Meanwhile, we'll get them started on *doing*. Ethics isn't just a subject area in a Jewish classroom. It's also a way of life, a way of responding to one another and to our families, community, and world. By giving students opportunities to put into practice the *mitzvot* they study, we present a defense of Jewish ethics more eloquent than any lecture. As our students experience the sweetness and dignity of a life guided by *mitzvot*, the value of those *mitzvot* becomes clear. They will do, and they will understand. (I can't resist the temptation to point out that the people of Israel's declaration that they will live by the *mitzvot* is recorded in Exodus 24:7. Twenty-four/seven—the very phrase our students use to describe something they do all the time. A slang-loving mystic could have a lot of fun with this one!)

In his *Ethics,* Aristotle warns that the study of ethics is inappropriate for young people. The theoretical issues underlying various systems of ethics may indeed be too subtle and complicated for young people to grasp. But Judaism says it's never too soon to introduce children to a life of *mitzvot.* We think of Shammai cutting a hole into the roof above his grandson's cradle, covering it with branches so the infant could observe the mitzvah of being in the sukkah. Did the baby understand the importance of the mitzvah, the significance of the holiday? Obviously, no. But the pattern of observance was set; the first step was taken; understanding would follow. In our classes, we too lay a foundation for a life enriched by *mitzvot* by combining theory and practice, and by adapting every lesson to accommodate our students' ages and levels of understanding. If we persevere, we can help our students come, eventually, to a joyous appreciation of their heritage. We help them experience—or reexperience, if you will—what it meant to stand at the foot of Sinai and hear the Law proclaimed.

It won't be easy. We may be troubled by our own reservations; we may have to deal with challenges presented by other religions and by a powerful popular culture. We will undoubtedly be frustrated by the challenges of trying to teach any complex subject to young, usually undisciplined minds. But the rewards of persevering are so great, the harvest that beckons us so sweet, that it more than justifies our labor.

* *The Early Years: Laying a Foundation*

We know that young students, even more than older ones, learn by doing; they're more likely to understand and remember concrete examples than abstract principles. During the elementary years, then, the study of ethics may focus on the discussion of specific *mitzvot,* particularly those students can practice in their daily lives. Respecting parents, being kind to animals, visiting the sick, contributing to *sh'lom bayit*—even the youngest children can understand the importance of such *mitzvot*. As teachers, we can help students find ways of putting these ideals into action. A lesson on *sh'lom bayit,* for example, may include assigning students to keep a log for a week and record in it one special thing they did each day to contribute to the peace and happiness of their families. Students can also make get-well cards for congregants who are ill or send holiday cards to those living in retirement homes. Elementary students (and older students as well) are sure to enjoy going on a field trip to an animal shelter and learning how to care for pets. If the staff at the shelter permits, students can show kindness to the animals there by helping to groom and feed them, cleaning cages, walking dogs, or simply playing with any animal longing for attention.

In our classrooms, we can find many ways to give students opportunities to practice a range of *mitzvot*. The chapter on Purim describes an activity for relating a discussion of *kavod* to agreeing on rules for classroom behavior. Those rules can reflect *mitzvot* such as *g'milut ḥasadim* (speaking kindly to one another, sharing supplies) and *bal tashḥit* (not scribbling in textbooks). From the first days of religious school, students can also be encouraged to make *tzedakah* a regular part of their lives and to understand that Judaism sees this mitzvah not as an option but as an obligation for every person trying to lead a good life. Students are more likely to find religious school *tzedakah* contributions meaningful if some of the money they contribute comes from their own earnings. If you send a letter to parents at the beginning of the year, you may want to suggest that they encourage their children to set aside part of their weekly allowances for *tzedakah*.

Holidays present more opportunities for learning about and practicing *mitzvot*. Many religious schools have Sukkot food drives to symbolically share the harvest with those served by community food banks. Young students may find bringing in non-perishable items for such drives even more concrete and rewarding than contributing money. If other teachers agree, an elementary class can take responsibility for sorting contributions and reporting on the drive's success to the rest of the school. Our school took a suggestion from a newsletter several years ago and now collects boxes of cereal during the seven weeks of counting the *Omer* to mark the grain harvest. Counting the cereal boxes brought in each week is a natural, enjoyable activity for young students, one that helps them more vividly imagine how helpful these *tzedakah* contributions will be to other children.

Holiday art projects can also encourage the practice of *mitzvot*. As Ḥanukkah approaches, students can make special *tzedakah* boxes to take home and place next to the family menorah, and can be encouraged to put some of the *gelt* they receive into those boxes. For Purim, students can make *mishlo'aḥ manot* for elderly congregation members or nursing home residents. If transportation challenges can be worked out, perhaps students can deliver the baskets in person. Such projects introduce students to the Jewish tradition of making the less fortunate part of every joyous occasion. We can also encourage students to share such activities with their parents, integrating *tzedakah* into their families' Jewish lives.

While students develop the habit of observing such traditions, they can also study texts and ideas on which those traditions are based. Often, the study of ethics can be integrated with other subjects. When they study Tanach stories, young students can explore *mitzvot* in more depth and get a sense of their complexity. For example, what does the story of Joseph and his brothers teach us about how parental favoritism and sibling rivalry endanger *sh'lom bayit*? When we read about Joseph's reunion with his brothers, what do we learn about justice, atonement, and forgiveness, and about how *sh'lom bayit* can be restored? A close study of the Ten Commandments can also be profitable for students this age. They will find it easy to relate some of the commandments to their everyday lives, to talk about how they can help to honor Shabbat and how they can show respect for their parents. Some of the other commandments may not seem so directly related to our students' lives, but we can help students find connections. A discussion of the third commandment, for example, may focus on the importance of keeping promises; a lesson on the ninth commandment may lead into a discussion of *l'shon hara*. The Book of Proverbs is another text that works well with young students, since it contains many short, relatively simple sayings for children to explore. Students may enjoy expressing their ideas about such texts in impromptu skits that apply ethical principles to everyday situations.

From such studies and activities, even very young students can start to understand central Jewish ethical teachings. From their own experiences, children learn that practicing *mitzvot* makes them feel better about themselves and that, young as they are, they can make a difference in the lives of their families and communities. Such simple but profound lessons lay the foundations for a lifetime of *mitzvot*, and for studies students will undertake and experiences they'll have as they continue through religious school.

✳ *The Middle Years: Growing in Understanding*

Middle school students can work toward both a fuller understanding of Jewish ethical principles and a still-deeper involvement in *tikkun olam*. The study of texts that inform Jewish ideas about ethics can continue as students learn about, for example, the teachings of the Prophets. While studying the stories of Isaiah, Amos, and other prophets, students can select favorite passages about peace and justice, then incorporate the verses into murals or collages. Devoting a few minutes each week to discussing the *haftarah* portion provides further opportunities to study the prophets' ethical teachings. Middle school students also benefit from returning to previously studied texts, exploring them in new ways and in more depth. Such lessons underscore the point that we never really finish reading our seminal texts, that we can always learn more if we return to them with new maturity, with fresh insights gained from new experiences. For example, middle school students reviewing the Ten Commandments might study them, this time, in the context of the Holiness Code. How do the verses of Leviticus 19 echo the Ten Commandments, commenting on and adding to them?

The middle years are also a good time to introduce students to some rabbinical writings. For example, learning about the eight levels of *tzedakah* set forth by Maimonides can move students toward a more mature understanding of why and how they should help others, and of ways in which the lives and feelings of both givers and recipients are affected by the manner in which *tzedakah* is practiced. If students then help plan *tzedakah* projects for the class or for the school as a whole, they will have a chance to apply what they have learned, to make sure that each project honors the mitzvah of *lo bushah* by respecting the pride and dignity of those it helps.

Pirkei Avot is another text that works well with students this age. Like Proverbs, it contains many short passages that, although richest if read in context, can also profitably be studied in isolation. Students get the benefit and excitement of reading an original text without feeling overwhelmed by complexity or sheer length. I like to observe the tradition of studying *Pirkei Avot* during the counting of the *Omer* by typing up a few sayings from the appropriate chapter each week and discussing them in class. Students will find many ideas that apply directly to their own lives in these sayings, and can also begin to get a sense of the personalities of some of our great rabbis and of some characteristics of rabbinic analysis. "Do not separate yourself from the community"; "You are not required to finish the work, but neither are you free to abstain from it"; "Who is wise? One who learns from all people." These and many other sayings can spark lively discussions among middle school students.

Middle school can also be a good time to introduce traditional and liberal Jewish concepts of *mitzvot*. If students attend public school, their friends will probably be asking them more and more questions about traditional Jewish practices: "Why don't Jews eat pork?" "Is it true you can't switch on a light on Saturdays, or even tear off a sheet of toilet paper?" Students who live in homes where these traditions are observed may be relatively well prepared to answer such questions, but even they may sometimes be reduced to saying, "I don't know. That's just what we do." Those who do not observe such traditions may be tempted to reply, "No, some Jews do weird stuff like that, but not my family—we do things the normal way." Neither answer gives our students' friends a positive impression of Judaism; more important, neither helps our students themselves regard their heritage and people with pride. Regardless of our school's affiliation, regardless of our own practices and beliefs, we need to help all our students understand various Jewish views of *mitzvot*.

The list of readings at the end of this chapter includes some books that can guide us as we help students develop this understanding. With middle school students, we can stress basic points: the idea that belief in the Covenant between God and the Jewish people has been fundamental to our religion since its beginning; the idea that Judaism sees the Torah not as a burden but as a gift; the idea that Jews throughout the centuries have worked hard to understand the laws in the Torah, and to live by them in ways that help us lead righteous lives that bring us closer to God.

We can admit that not all Jews agree about the origin of the Torah or how to interpret the laws it contains; but we also can make it clear that all Jews *do* agree that the Torah is precious and important, and that studying its laws helps us become better people. We can introduce concepts such as building a fence around the Torah, show students how these concepts have been applied, and explain why some Jews object to them. We can acknowledge that some approaches to Judaism stress ritual more than others, but emphasize that all branches of Judaism stress the absolute necessity of ethical behavior; we can trace back to the Prophets the admonition that ritual observance has little merit unless it's part of a life of righteous action. We can, I think, refute with utter conviction the view that any branch of Judaism is obsessed with law but indifferent to matters of the spirit or to the need to make the world a better place.

If we can help our middle school students grasp this much, and can further help them understand how different branches of Judaism arrive at their interpretations of *mitzvot*, we'll accomplish a great deal. If we also help our students regard all these ways of interpreting *mitzvot* with respect, we will, in my opinion, accomplish still more. I've heard an Orthodox teacher dismiss Reform Judaism as "pick-and-choose Judaism," telling his students that liberal approaches to interpreting *mitzvot* amount to little more than rationalizations for ignorance and laziness. I've also heard Reform teachers caricature Orthodox Judaism as a dying system blind both to the insights of Biblical scholarship and to the suffering in the world, more concerned about saying the proper blessing over each morsel of food than about reaching out to feed the hungry. I think it's a shame. We're carefully respectful when we teach our students about Christianity and Islam. If we could be equally careful and show equal respect when we teach them about other branches of Judaism, what vital work we could do for the mitzvah of *klal Yisra'el*.

Naturally, we will emphasize the understandings of *mitzvot* that we ourselves accept, and that our synagogue or school endorses. But it's not unreasonable to think that we can also find at least a little time to introduce students to the views held by other branches of Judaism. All of these views are, after all, a part of the history of the Jewish people; our students cannot be well informed about Judaism if they are ignorant about what other Jews believe and why. And while it is natural and appropriate for us to advocate our own views and those of our synagogue or school, it's not unreasonable to think we can treat all views with respect. I've taught at a Reform religious school, at an Orthodox day school, and at two religious schools that tried to meet the needs and respect the beliefs of all the Jews in the small communities they served. In all of these schools, the students have been full of questions about their brothers and sisters in other synagogues and temples; when I've answered their questions honestly and tactfully, stressing underlying similarities as well as important differences, the students have invariably responded well. I don't think their pride in their own beliefs was the least bit compromised by my suggestion that they regard others' beliefs with tolerance and respect. Some day, our students will be serving together on the boards of Jewish community centers and Jewish charities, of Zionist organizations and organizations that promote social justice. Is it not our duty to prepare students to work together harmoniously, to overcome divisiveness and build the solidarity of the Jewish people? How can our efforts to increase understanding among all denominations be anything but a force for good in the lives of Jews here, in Israel, and throughout the world?

As we continue to teach our students about *mitzvot* and to exemplify their principles through our own words and actions, we can also look for additional ways to help our students incorporate into their own lives the practice of *mitzvot*. During the bar/bat mitzvah year, for example, classes may consider making *tzedakah* part of their observance of this milestone. With our guidance and encouragement, individual students or the class as a whole may decide to give some portion of the gifts they receive to a cause of their choice. Some students may forgo gifts altogether and enclose contribution envelopes with their invitations, asking family and friends to mail in contributions instead of buying presents.

It's important to get parents' support before proposing such a project; judging from my experience, such support isn't hard to secure. Students may show some initial reluctance, but they too can get caught up in the idea of marking their transition to religious adulthood by making a significant contribution to a cause they recognize as worthwhile. And it's fascinating and heartwarming to see our students' personalities and commitments reflected in the causes they choose. Just recently, I received a bar mitzvah invitation from a former student and was charmed by the printed notice included in the envelope. In honor of Tovia's bar mitzvah, the notice said, his parents are making a contribution to Mazon, and Tovia himself has decided to donate a portion of his gifts to the Cat Welfare Society of Israel. Well, of course. Tovia has always adored cats—when one of his beloved pets passed away a few years ago, he saved up to plant a tree in Israel in her memory. How sweet and fitting it is that he's using his bar mitzvah as another opportunity to show both his loyalty to Israel and his concern for the animals that are so special to him. When we encourage our students to take advantage of such opportunities, we help them form the habit of finding meaningful ways to share the joy of their life-cycle celebrations.

We can also encourage students to move from occasional *tzedakah* projects to doing volunteer work on a regular basis. Volunteer opportunities for middle school students are admittedly limited: Some community agencies, lacking the staff to supervise young volunteers, turn them away. Others accept middle school volunteers if they'll do humble chores such as raking leaves and washing windows. In addition, many nursing homes welcome middle school visitors who will chat with residents or provide simple services, and some after school programs for immigrant and refugee children can use middle school students as readers. If we believe that any work is dignified and meaningful if it meets the needs of the less fortunate, we'll probably, with perseverance and ingenuity, be able to help students find volunteer jobs that benefit their community and build their own conviction that they can and should work to make things better.

✳ *High School: Affirming Commitments*

During the final years of religious school, class discussions may frequently focus on applying Jewish ethical teachings to contemporary issues and to choices students are making in their personal lives. It isn't hard to get young people talking about such topics. Many students are surprised and excited to learn classic Jewish texts actually address such subjects as gossip, shopping, and tattoos; many find it cool that Talmudic principles can be applied to situations they encounter in real life, such as returning lost possessions and determining responsibility for accidental damages. One teacher stimulates interest in such discussions by writing short narratives based on cases drawn from the Talmud and using his students' names for the parties involved: "Rachel tells her father that she'll clean the garage but later realizes that she doesn't have time. Todd offers to clean it for her, and she agrees. But Todd spills some oil on the floor, and when Ben comes running into the garage later, he slips on the oil and breaks his leg. Who is responsible for Ben's injury—Ben himself? Todd? Rachel? Rachel's father?" Students get passionately involved as they role-play the parts assigned to them, making arguments on their own behalf; the other students in the class act as judges, referring to Talmudic principles described in the textbook to resolve the dilemma.

One challenge we face in such classes is keeping Jewish texts and ideas at the center of discussion, rather than just using them as introductory devices. Most students will be happy to tell stories about the times they dented the family car (although it wasn't really their fault), describe the gross tattoos they've seen on other students, or explain why they repeated a rumor that a teacher was visiting pornographic websites during study hall.

Getting students to take a serious look at these actions in the context of Jewish principles, and perhaps to admit that they should take responsibility for a problem or that their behavior fell short of the mark, can be more difficult. The temptation to get completely caught up in the fun of trading personal anecdotes is strong, and the stock answers for resolving any ethical issue are always readily available: "Well, it's not something *I* would do, personally, but if that's his choice, who's to say he's wrong?" "Maybe some people wouldn't agree, but *I'm* the one who's most affected by it, so it's *my* decision." Even if they are impressed that rabbis centuries ago discussed the dangers of gossip, students aren't likely to admit that their actions and opinions should be limited by Jewish wisdom and authority. It goes too much against the grain in times when nearly all television shows and popular songs, and quite a few widely respected experts, assure young people that they themselves are the best judges of their own actions, and that deferring to any authority would mean compromising their individuality.

There's no simple, guaranteed approach to getting students to see past such attitudes, but it sometimes helps to challenge their assumptions directly. Most students have never had to defend the idea that there are no objective standards of right and wrong, or that all opinions are equally valid. Indeed, many students have never heard a full argument defending such beliefs; they've merely heard the opinions asserted, and accepted them because they're popular and convenient. If we challenge students about their fundamental assumptions—if, for example, we ask them to defend the idea that personal choices are merely "personal," and that families, communities, laws, and traditions don't have to be taken into consideration when we make "personal" decisions—we may at least raise some doubts. We may at least reduce the authority of assumptions many students accept without question, creating room for more complex, demanding ideas about right and wrong.

It may also help if our discussions focus not only on analyzing specific ethical choices but also on identifying and articulating underlying, distinctive principles of Jewish approaches to ethics. If we continually stress these principles—for example, that life is precious and meant to be cherished and enjoyed, that human beings do indeed have the freedom and the ability to choose what is good, that all share the responsibility to protect the weak, that the rights of the individual must be balanced against the rights and needs of the community—students may come to see the beauty of these principles and to acknowledge their truth. So many forces today endorse the natural impulse to selfishness, encouraging our students to be cool to the point of being callous. But when students encounter a teacher who isn't embarrassed to argue that there can and should be something higher and nobler to life, something inside them stirs. They may not always admit it—at least not explicitly, not immediately, not publicly. That might not seem cool. But I truly believe our efforts, and our example, will eventually make a difference in the lives of our students—sometimes a slight difference, sometimes a decisive one, but a difference. The belief that we can, in fact, make at least a slight difference, and the hope that we can sometimes make a decisive one, will sustain us despite all frustrations and apparent failures, will keep us teaching.

High school students may also find individual or group research projects challenging and satisfying, and we can find ways to link those projects to the study of ethics. For example, students can use the Internet and print resources to research prominent Jews, past and present, whose lives have been shaped by *mitzvot* such as *ometz lev* (Hannah Senesh), *rofeh ḥolim* (Jonas Salk), and *piku'aḥ nefesh* (Henrietta Szold). Students can then share what they have learned with the rest of the class, or perhaps make presentations at an assembly for the entire school. Students may also explore the ethical teachings of thinkers such as Martin Buber or Elie Wiesel. The insights students gain from such research will enrich classroom discussions of ethical issues.

In addition to encouraging students to explore ethical principles, we can give them opportunities to act on those principles by encouraging them to continue their individual volunteer efforts and to undertake special mitzvah projects as a group. Either on their own or in cooperation with the youth group, high school classes can undertake projects that benefit the congregation—planning and leading children's services for the High Holy Days, cleaning a storage area, taking responsibility for keeping a current-events bulletin board up to date. These students can become actively involved in the life of the religious school by writing personal notes to welcome new kindergarten students and by serving on panels to give advice to students getting ready for their *b'nei mitzvah*. With guidance from experienced teachers and from the religious school director, high school students can prepare and present lessons for younger classes, and also help plan assemblies and family-education events. Such experiences introduce students to the joys of teaching and prepare them for the mitzvah of sharing what they have learned.

High school students can also take leadership roles in deciding how the school's *tzedakah* contributions are used. In our congregation, for example, the contributions from the first half of the year always go to a community agency, the contributions from the second half to a Jewish cause. All the students vote on where the funds will go; the oldest class has the responsibility of presenting the younger classes with options. High school students visit community agencies, collect brochures, and, when possible, volunteer at least on a temporary basis; they visit the websites of Jewish organizations, request literature, and sometimes make phone calls to get more information. Twice a year, at assemblies of the full school, these older students present the results of their research, making arguments on behalf of the causes they favor before other students vote. Getting busy high school students to do such research can be a pain; often, their teachers and I tire of nagging them and consider how much quicker it would be to do the research ourselves. But when we persevere, and when we hear teenagers explain, clearly and passionately, just why it's important to support the Ronald McDonald House or an agency that provides blind Israelis with guide dogs that respond to Hebrew, we know our nagging paid off. We know our students have taken yet another step toward a full, active commitment to the ethical principles that will guide them as Jewish adults.

✳ *First Fruits, Inheritances, and Choices*

Just as it's a fortunate, fascinating coincidence that Rosh Hashanah falls at the beginning of the religious school year, it's fortunate and fascinating that the end of most religious school years usually coincides with Shavuot. How appropriate it is to conclude a year's work with a celebration of first fruits. As we attend confirmations or end-of-year assemblies, we can rejoice in thinking about what students learned during our year together. True, this isn't yet a full harvest—even for students who are completing their religious school education, there are still so many texts to study, still so many issues to explore and resolve. Characters are still not fully formed, and many commitments are still tentative. But any harvest is worth celebrating. As we look back on the year, we're bound to recall frustrations we endured, lessons we never got to, topics we really should have covered. Shavuot reminds us we should also think about what we have in fact accomplished. We shouldn't dismiss this harvest because it isn't yet complete. Any progress our students made during the year is good in itself; it also prepares the ground for what is still to come.

It's also fortunate and fascinating that Shavuot has come to be a celebration of the *mitzvot,* and that it's marked by reading both the account of the Revelation at Sinai and the Book of Ruth. So much of the work we do in religious school involves encouraging our students to learn about and live by the *mitzvot;* how appropriate it is to end our year by expressing our gratitude for the ideas that have helped generations of Jews lead better, holier lives. What could be more fitting than to end a year of study by joining with our students to remember the day when, according to tradition, we, our ancestors, and our descendants all stood at Sinai together to receive the *mitzvot* for the first time?

But Ruth's ancestors weren't at Sinai—at least, not her physical ancestors. Ruth accepted the *mitzvot* not because she'd inherited them from her parents and grandparents but because she chose them for herself. The traditions she'd inherited told her to return to her Moabite gods; she broke from that inheritance to live by the *mitzvot,* to follow a higher, more difficult path.

Probably, all our students are in religious school because they've inherited Judaism from at least one parent. Even so, all our students have at least one thing in common with Ruth: They have other choices available to them. Even if their ancestry on both sides stretches clear back to Abraham, our students don't have to be Jews unless they choose to do so. Other religions would welcome them eagerly, and secular culture is always ready to absorb them. In a free and open society, the choice to remain Jewish cannot be taken for granted, will not happen by default. Our students are fully aware of their other options; they feel the allure of those options every day. They don't have to stay Jewish unless, like Ruth, they choose to live by the *mitzvot,* to accept the gift offered at Sinai.

By helping our students see that the *mitzvot* are indeed a gift and not a burden, we help them make that choice. Our students' freedom to follow other paths makes our work more difficult but also more important. It intensifies our efforts, and increases our joy at every sign of harvest. It makes us even more determined to help our students know why they should accept the inheritance given to their ancestors when they stood at Sinai, hearing the *mitzvot* proclaimed amid thunder and lightning; it motivates us to help our students make the same choice Ruth made when she stood at the crossroad between Moab and Israel, listening to the promptings of a still, small voice.

SUGGESTED RESOURCES

Abba Hillel Silver, *Where Judaism Differed: An Inquiry into the Distinctiveness of Judaism* (New York: Macmillan, 1956).

This classic work can be an invaluable resource as we teach our students about Jewish ethics. Drawing on hundreds of Jewish texts, and also on many texts from other religions, Rabbi Silver argues that Judaism's insistence on the need to live an ethical life is our religion's defining characteristic. He identifies underlying Jewish moral principles, explains how they differ from those of other religions, and responds eloquently to those who criticize Jewish ideas about ethics as inadequate or inferior. This profound, beautifully written book fills us with pride in our heritage, and shows us that our pride has an unshakable foundation.

Milton Steinberg, *Basic Judaism* (New York: Harcourt, 1947).

This is the first adult-oriented book about Judaism I ever read, and it's still one of the texts I consult most often. Among the sections most relevant to the themes of this chapter are those explaining traditionalist and modernist views of Torah and Revelation. I find Rabbi Steinberg's discussion both perceptive and balanced, presented so clearly that we can share at least some of his ideas with our students. The sections on "The Good Life" and "Israel and the Nations" can also be very useful as we help our students understand distinctive characteristics of Judaism and Jewish ethics.

⬛❋ WEBSITE ⬛

National Association of Temple Educators | **www.rj.org/nate**

This website for the National Association of Temple Educators, an organization for Reform religious school teachers, provides links to descriptions of *tikkun olam* and *tzedakah* programs that have been successfully implemented at schools and synagogues across North America. The descriptions tell you how to get further information from the educators who have created programs such as Adopt a Righteous Gentile, Environmental Family Day, and I Shared My Birthday.

7. Conclusion: Shabbat

THE JEWISH EDUCATOR'S SUMMER

Several years ago, on the last day of religious school, I decided to devote my final hour with my fourth-graders to reviewing what we'd learned. It had been a good year; we'd learned a lot. For once, we'd finished our Hebrew textbook. And in addition to discussing *Tanach* stories and holidays, we'd studied about a dozen *mitzvot* in depth. We'd begin our review, I decided, by going over those *mitzvot* one last time, starting with the very first one we'd studied. We'd lingered over this one for several weeks, creating a bulletin board together, doing homework assignments, relating it to *Tanach* stories, and having many lively discussions. They'll remember plenty about this one, I thought, and introduced the topic confidently.

"We've studied a number of *mitzvot* together this year," I said, "including one that can and should be part of our lives every day. Will someone get us started by sharing thoughts about why *sh'lom bayit* is important?"

The students stared. They fidgeted. They did not speak. Impossible, I thought. They can't have forgotten *this* one—*bal tashḥit*, maybe, but not *this* one. Maybe they just didn't like the way I worded the question. I tried again.

"Will someone get us started," I asked, "by reminding us about what *sh'lom bayit* is?"

Probably, they didn't really start sweating at that point; probably, that's a detail memory has added. But they definitely looked uncomfortable, and about as lost as any human beings can be. Impossible as it seemed, it had to be true. They'd forgotten. They weren't just being stubborn or lazy. These were sweet, smart kids, and we'd had a good year. Clearly, they wanted to please me by answering my question. But they just couldn't do it.

Oh, well, I told myself staunchly. September was a long time ago, and we've studied so many *mitzvot*—probably, they've all just blended together in the students' minds. A hint or two should get them going, especially since we've had such a successful year with Hebrew. After all, both *shalom* and *bayit* had been vocabulary words in the first chapter in our textbook.

"Let's figure it out," I said. "What does *bayit* mean? We learned it the first week, and we've used it often. Come on, now. *Bayit*. What does it mean?"

They concentrated fiercely, looking thoroughly miserable, and finally one girl grimaced and raised her hand. "'House,' maybe?" she tried.

"Excellent!" I said, amazed that only one student remembered. "That's exactly right—*bayit* means 'house.' And I *know* you know what *shalom* means."

This time, the whole class chanted readily, "Hello, goodbye, peace."

"Very good!" I said. "Now, just put it together—*shalom* and *bayit*. We did a bulletin board about it, you kept journals about it, we discussed it many times. *Sh'lom bayit*. What does it mean?"

Silence. And then enlightenment dawned in the face of one of my brightest students. Eagerly, he thrust his hand into the air. "I know, I know!" he cried. "It means 'Goodbye, house!'"

This is why Jewish educators need summer vacations. We all know patience is a mandatory mitzvah for teachers. Hillel demonstrated that decisively when he gave a patiently brilliant answer to the man who demanded to be taught the whole Torah in moments. Hillel could have just shoved him over—the guy was standing on one foot, after all; what a tempting target he must have made. But Hillel was patient, and we know we must be, too: as Hillel himself tells us in *Pirkei Avot*, the hot-tempered cannot teach. Even a teacher's patience, however, has limits. If Hillel had been meeting with our students once or twice or three times a week since September, even he would need a break by May. All teachers need to get away from the day-to-day demands of preparing and presenting lessons, to have some significant time off to think back on the last year and get ready for the next one.

The same sort of wisdom is embedded in Shabbat. No matter how important our work is, no matter how much we love it or how rewarding we find it, we need time to rest. But not just to rest—Shabbat, ideally, involves more than simply taking a day off. All four of the Torah's references to Shabbat emphasize the basic point that we should rest and not work, but some also tell us to "observe" or "honor" Shabbat, to keep it holy. Over the millennia, we've come to think of Shabbat not only as a day of rest but also as a day for being with family, for studying, for experiencing deep joy, and for discovering new levels of peace. If we think of summer vacation as the Jewish educator's special Shabbat, perhaps we can make this time, too, not only a time of rest that gives us a break from work but also a time of rest that prepares us to begin again.

✳ *Shabbat Blessings*

We observe and honor Shabbat when we come together in synagogue to pray, to study, and to feel once again that we are part of a community transcending the secular workplaces and schools where most of us spend most of our week, a community transcending space and time. We can observe and honor Shabbat when we lie down, when we rise up, when we walk on our way. But it is in our homes that we experience Shabbat most profoundly, when we gather at our tables on Friday night with those we love most. We say blessings over the candles, the wine, the bread. And we ask God to bless our children.

During the academic year, we spend a lot of time focusing on other people's children. We prepare lessons for them, think up ways to praise and reward them, worry about them, sometimes lie awake at night trying to figure out ways to reach them. Most Jewish teachers have day jobs that take up much of our time, then devote part of our afternoons, evenings, or weekends—time we'd otherwise spend with our own families or friends—to our classes. We don't have to feel bad about making this choice. On the contrary, we should feel good about it. Teaching other people's children is sacred work, work that must be done to help the Jewish people survive. But sometimes we may worry that our own children—or spouses, or friends—may feel left out or are not getting all the attention and care we'd give them if we didn't give so much to our students.

Summer can be a time of compensating for the hours we spend away from our loved ones during the academic year, of focusing more sharply on the people who mean the most to us. We can make the time usually dedicated to religious school into time devoted to family or friends. If we teach on Sunday mornings and often end up tossing our children slices of half-toasted bread as we herd them through the door, telling them that they can eat in the car and that they're better off without butter anyhow because it's loaded with cholesterol, we can make summer Sundays a time for leisurely pancake breakfasts and for chatting about plans for the coming week. Maybe we can go to the zoo or give the dog that long walk in the country he's been craving all year. If we teach on Wednesday evenings, we can make summer Wednesdays a time for serving pizza or some other family favorite and then playing a game, watching a video, or going for a bike ride together. Any shared activity, however simple, makes the point—to our family and friends, and to ourselves—that we're reveling in the extra opportunity to be together.

Chances are, we haven't really neglected our families and friends during the academic year. Most religious school teachers I know aren't the sorts to neglect anybody. They just have a marvelous knack for making time expand, for packing more into a day than most people can. But they also tend to be supremely conscientious, prone to feeling guilty whenever they have to say "no" to anybody, no matter how often they've said "yes." Summer can be a time for setting our minds at ease by making special efforts to focus even more attention on our loved ones, for easing the perceptions of neglect that can sometimes develop. Like Shabbat, summer can be a time for savoring the special blessings of home, of gathering together, of making explicit the love and appreciation we in fact feel every day of the week, every week of the year.

✳ *Shabbat Study, Shabbat Joy*

Shabbat is a time not only of rest but also of study—but not the kind of study we associate with homework and tests. Shabbat is a time for studying things we love because we love them, of reading Torah and other Jewish texts on our own or in informal groups where no one is taking attendance or giving out grades. On Shabbat, we learn because we choose to learn, free of the pressures that almost always develop in academic settings. The satisfactions of this sort of learning can be an important part of the joy we find in Shabbat.

For teachers, summer, like Shabbat, can be a time to delight in study. We don't have lessons to prepare, so we can take some time to read—to actually read whole books, not just to just look something up, not just to skim a chapter to prepare for class. And we can choose the things we read. During the academic year, we spend a lot of time with textbooks written for young people. We may find these textbooks charming and enjoyable, and we're almost bound to learn something new from them at least once in a while. But they were written for our students, not for us; we have needs such texts can't satisfy and questions they can't answer. Of course, many of us find time to read some Jewish books written for adults even during the academic year. But if we've had to subordinate our desire to learn to the need to get ready to teach, summer can be a chance to put our own educational needs first.

True, even during the summer, we'll feel tempted to think of our students. There's that book on learning disorders we really ought to read because we'll have a student with dyslexia in class next fall; there's the ad we've saved for months, describing a book on how to teach *mitzvot*—maybe this is the time to finally place an order; or we'll be teaching a high school class for the first time next year, doing a new unit on the history of Zionism—we should find books that can give us some background. For Jewish educators, this sort of summer reading is often necessary and always commendable.

But I'd like to suggest that we do another sort of summer reading as well. I'd like to suggest that, at some point during the summer, we read at least one Jewish book that has nothing to do with the subjects we'll teach in the fall or the challenges we'll encounter. At some point during the summer, let's each try to read at least one Jewish book simply because it sounds like fun—perhaps a biography of a Jewish leader who has always fascinated us, a mystery novel with a Jewish detective, a book on Jewish mysticism so esoteric our students couldn't fathom even one page, a collection of Jewish humor. Whatever it is, it should be something we choose not because we think it will help us do a better job in the classroom but simply because we want to read it for its own sake, for our own sake.

If we read at least one such book over the summer, we can make summer, like Shabbat, a time for increasing our own knowledge of Judaism. Summer can be a time to experience the joys we so often describe to our students—the joys of encountering new ideas, people, places, and times; of struggling to understand something we find truly challenging; of reawakening and satisfying our curiosity. If we come to our classrooms in September fresh from the delights of learning, invigorated by the challenge of stretching our own minds and the opportunity to explore our own interests, we stand a much better chance of helping our students get excited about the year ahead. We'll be more persuasive advocates for the joy of learning if we've just experienced that joy ourselves.

✳ *Shabbat Shalom*

The rest from work and worry and effort and disappointment, the blessings of family and friends, the joys of study—all of these are important elements of Shabbat. Together, they help us find Shabbat peace.

Summer, like Shabbat, can give us distance from the worthwhile but wearying tasks that absorb so much of our time. It can help us put our successes and failures into perspective. It can help us build the energy, and the courage, to begin again.

When my student offered his definition of *sh'lom bayit,* I managed to hold things together a little longer. I smiled, shook my head regretfully, told him his answer wasn't quite exactly right, and gave more hints, eventually prodding someone into answering correctly. We got through the rest of the *mitzvot,* finished our review, and went downstairs to join the other classes for the end-of-year assembly. As principal, I made my speech about what a good year it had been; praised the students and gave them their certificates of achievement; thanked the teachers and gave them their small gifts; mingled with the parents afterwards and told them what a delight it was to work with their children. We cleared away the remnants of bagels and cream cheese, poured out the last of the coffee, refrigerated the leftover juice, cleaned the kitchen, took out the garbage. And then my family got into the car, my husband pulled away from the curb, and I lost it.

I am wasting my life with these kids, I said, not softly. I plan, I work as hard as I can, I try again and again—and in the end, it all comes to nothing. "Goodbye, house"—after everything I did to get that one simple lesson across, that's what they think *sh'lom bayit* means. "Goodbye, house!" Either I'm incapable of teaching, or they're incapable of learning—maybe both. Either way, I've had it. I am never setting foot in a classroom again. And this time, I mean it.

My family listened silently, not trying to console me or reason with me. They're good that way. And they'd heard me say pretty much the same thing before—not at quite that volume, perhaps, but pretty much the same sentiments. From time to time, we'd heard my husband make similar speeches—he teaches, too. So we just finished the drive home, carried in our book bags, and got started on our summer.

It was a good summer. We rested, we spent some extra time together, we read books and articles we wanted to read and enjoyed telling one another about them. My family did help me put together a few religious school events—Summer Sundays, we call them—but they were relaxed, informal mornings for doing art projects, singing Israeli songs, playing Jewish charades, meeting at the Ronald McDonald House to wash windows and bake cookies for the residents. It was fun to see my students at these gatherings, to chat with them about vacations and camps and swimming lessons. From time to time, students would surprise me by referring to a discussion we'd had last year, using a Hebrew phrase we'd learned, saying they were following the suggestion to put aside part of the summer's allowance or earnings for *tzedakah*. At some point during the summer, the president of the congregation phoned and asked if I'd volunteer as principal for another year. Of course I will, I said, not taking even a moment to think it over. I'd be honored. And I also want to teach a class, and so does my husband.

Toward the end of August, we loaded up the car and pulled out of the driveway to start our family vacation. It was a happy moment; even so, we all felt a bit somber because just an hour ago we'd committed our pets to a brief stay in the kennel we knew they hated. And then, when we reached the street, my younger daughter rolled down her window, stuck out her head, and started waving frantically. "Goodbye, house!" she cried.

It took the rest of us a moment to catch on; but then we all laughed, rolled down our windows, and waved. "Goodbye, house!" we called out. *"Shalom, bayit!"*

We didn't have a candle in the car, or wine, or a spice box. Somehow, though, it felt like *havdalah*. We knew that we'd had a good rest, that we'd found our peace. We were ready to start again.

Appendix

◼◼◼ DISCUSSION QUESTIONS & ACTIVITIES ◼◼◼
FOR FACULTY DEVELOPMENT

Some religious school teachers might find it helpful to read chapters from this book, then meet to discuss them, either informally or as part of a regular faculty development program. The questions and activities below provide some suggestions for getting discussions started. The questions can be adapted to meet the needs of particular schools and particular teachers.

◢ CHAPTER 1

The Fall Holidays:
Looking Back, Setting Goals, and Moving Ahead

1. Take a few moments to jot down some notes about last year's high points and low points. If you taught religious school last year, you may want to focus on classroom experiences; if this is the first time you've taught religious school, you may want to focus on experiences in another job, with family and friends, or in some other setting that seems relevant. You may want to make lists of last year's successes and disappointments, of times when things worked out as planned and times when they didn't, of those moments when you felt satisfied and those when you felt frustrated.

2. The person leading this session may invite you to share some items from your lists with the group. If you prefer to keep some items on your lists private, that's your choice.

3. After looking over your own lists and listening to other teachers' comments, do you see any patterns that may help explain why some lessons and approaches were more successful than others? What conclusions can you draw?

4. What are your goals for this coming year in religious school? Think about both specific goals and broader, more general ones.

   ■ Do you feel that you understand the goals set by your school's curriculum? Would it help to have any of them clarified further? Do you have any insights about the curriculum that you wish to share with the other teachers?

   ■ How has looking back on the past year and listening to other teachers' comments affected your goals for the coming year? What kinds of successes do you hope to repeat and build on? What do you hope to do differently?

   ■ What are your academic goals for the coming year? What knowledge do you want your students to gain? What insights will you help them develop? What skills should they acquire or improve by the end of the year?

   ■ In what ways do you hope to encourage your students to grow emotionally and spiritually this year? What attitudes, habits, and feelings do you want to help them develop?

■ What are your personal goals for the coming year of religious school? What do you hope to learn from your experiences with your students? How do you hope to grow intellectually, spiritually, and emotionally?

5. Please share some of your thoughts about exchanging forgiveness with others during the Days of Awe.

■ Can you describe some of your experiences with exchanging forgiveness, or any customs you and your family have adopted?

■ Traditionally, Judaism favors face-to-face, one-on-one exchanges of forgiveness—do you agree that this is the best approach?

■ Might you and the religious school benefit if you used the Days of Awe to exchange forgiveness with other teachers or with other members of the congregation?

6. What is your approach to getting your classroom ready for a new year? What sort of atmosphere do you try to create? Do you think the physical appearance of the classroom has a significant effect on students' experiences in religious school?

7. The section on Simḥat Torah presents one view of the religious school teacher's role and symbolic importance. How do you see your role as a religious school teacher? How do you hope your students and the congregation as a whole will see you?

CHAPTER 2

Ḥanukkah: Building Jewish Identity

1. Think back to your own childhood and adolescence.

   ■ If you grew up as a Jew, did you experience tensions and doubts regarding your Jewish identity—at school, with friends, with family? How did you address those tensions and doubts? What influences strengthened your sense of Jewish identity?

   ■ If you're a Jew by choice, did you experience tensions and doubts regarding your religious identity as you were growing up? How did you address those tensions and doubts? If you like, you might also talk about some of the influences that eventually drew you to Judaism and helped you develop a sense of identity as a Jew.

2. Drawing on your own experiences, suggest ways in which individual teachers and the religious school as a whole might help students develop a strong sense of Jewish identity. Describe any lessons or activities you have used to help your students become modern Maccabees who take pride in their Judaism.

3. In your community, are there groups or organizations that offer a particular challenge for students trying to develop a Jewish identity? For example, are there any groups that are known for attempting to attract and convert young Jews? Please share any information or experiences you might have.

4. Discuss your students' tastes in music, movies, television, and other forms of popular culture. Do you see popular culture's influence on your students as primarily negative or primarily positive? In your classes, how have you tried to deal with the effects of popular culture?

5. Please share ideas about how to get parents involved with their children's religious education. Have you found effective ways of encouraging parents to participate in discussions or other class activities? Do you have any experiences with school-wide family-education events, or any ideas for kinds of programs your school might try?

6. What can we do to strengthen our students' sense of being a part of the Jewish people—within our individual classrooms, in the school as a whole, in our synagogue, in our city or town? How can we help our students develop ties to Jews in other parts of the country and around the world? Please share the approaches and activities you have tried in your classroom. Work with other teachers to generate new ideas about how you can cooperate to build students' sense of Jewish community.

7. Religious school teachers can be important role models for their students. In what ways do you attempt to set a positive example of Jewish adulthood—in what you say, in what you do, in other ways?

⚘ CHAPTER 3

Tu B'Shevat: Planting, Nurturing, Blossoming

1. The chapter says that it's often good to have a central theme for a class session. Do you agree that having a unifying theme is important, or do you prefer to cover a variety of topics without necessarily trying to relate them? What techniques have you used to help make class sessions unified?

2. Do your classes tend to follow a consistent pattern? That is, do you cover the same subjects in the same order or use some other method of giving each session the same structure? Or do you prefer to vary the order and structure more, to let classes unfold more spontaneously? What are some of the advantages and disadvantages of each approach?

3. Please share some of your favorite ways to open a class session. Are there techniques or rituals you use regularly? If so, how are they related to Jewish ideas and traditions, or to the content you're covering in class this year?

4. What do you do when a discussion lags because students don't respond to questions or offer opinions about a topic you introduce? Do you have favorite techniques you can recommend?

5. With one other teacher, or with a small group, brainstorm about ways to combine a variety of teaching methods in presenting a lesson about Israel. First, agree on a focus for the lesson—for example, early Zionist leaders, the kibbutz, or ethnic groups in Israel. Next, talk about what your goals for the lesson would be. How could you

incorporate several methods and approaches into a lesson about this topic? How could you combine full-class discussions, small-group activities, and individual work? How could you include the arts, games, snacks, and so on? How would you adapt the lesson to suit students of different ages? Please share your ideas with the full group.

6. Do you have a particular approach to ending a class session? How do you keep the last minutes of a class productive and pleasant? How is your approach to handling the end of class rooted in Jewish ideas and traditions?

✂ CHAPTER 4

Purim: Teaching as Celebration

1. What role should the arts play in Jewish education? Do you find the arts a valuable complement to academic instruction, or do you think our limited time with students could more profitably be spent in other ways?

2. What sorts of art projects have worked well with your classes? What advice can you give other teachers?

3. How do you incorporate music into your classes? If your school has a music teacher, do you work together to decide what songs should be taught and how they should be taught? If there is no specialist, what approaches have you tried on your own?

4. Do you use informal or formal dramatics in your classes? What frustrations or successes have you experienced?

5. Have you invited guests to help in classes incorporating the arts? What have your experiences been, and what advice can you offer?

6. Do you have favorite games that you use to help students learn or review material? How do you keep all students involved and minimize problems associated with competition?

7. What classroom management problems do you encounter most often? How do you handle them?

8. Do you agree with the approach to discipline presented in this chapter? What reservations or additional suggestions do you have?

✳ CHAPTER 5

Passover: Four Lessons from a Classic Textbook

1. What are some of your favorite techniques for stimulating students to ask questions?

2. Describe the kinds of questions you most often ask in class. What goals do you have in mind when you ask different sorts of questions? It has often been said that the kinds of questions we ask determine the kinds of answers we receive. Do you agree with that statement?

3. What do you do when a student asks a question you can't answer? If a student catches a teacher in a mistake, how should the teacher respond?

4. Do you agree that Jewish history should be an important part of the curriculum? What is your approach to teaching this subject area?

5. How would you define the relationship between the school and the home? How can the religious school and the home be partners in a student's Jewish education?

6. If you are a parent yourself, what sorts of support and encouragement do you want the religious school to provide for your family? What sorts of family-education efforts have helped you most as a parent?

7. How do you handle the challenge of teaching topics—for example, the holidays—that students have often studied before? How do you keep familiar material from getting repetitious and boring for the students—and for you?

✳ CHAPTER 6

Shavuot: Celebrating a Life of Mitzvot

1. Approaches to teaching *mitzvot* and ideas about Revelation will vary depending on our students' ages. What approach do you take with your students? What topics have proven especially challenging? How have you handled these challenges?

2. What are your own beliefs about Revelation? How do those beliefs influence your approach to teaching various parts of the curriculum—for example, *Tanach*, holidays, ethics?

3. Are there particular ethical principles or *mitzvot* that you consider especially important for students in the age group you teach? How have you tried to emphasize these principles or *mitzvot* with your students?

4. This chapter argues that we can present all Jewish views of *mitzvot* and Revelation as worthy of respect, even if we don't endorse those views ourselves. Do you agree, or do you find some approaches to Judaism so objectionable that you feel obliged to present them in a more critical light? For example, one teacher responded to a draft of this chapter by saying, "Our students have so little time in our religious school; I want to spend that time teaching my students who they are, not who they are not or who they are in comparison to others. Many 'traditional' teachings are derogatory to my brand of Judaism." Do you agree or disagree with this teacher's views?

5. Some religions reject Jewish ideas about the need to order our lives by *mitzvot*, and so do ways of thinking such as moral relativism. Have you encountered such attitudes from your students? If so, how have you responded?

6. What *tzedakah* or other mitzvah projects have worked especially well with your students? Are there special projects or new emphases that you'd like to encourage the school as a whole to consider?

7. If you've tried to involve your students in volunteer work or community service, please comment on the successes and frustrations you've encountered. What advice can you offer to other teachers who want to encourage their students to explore such opportunities?

Index